Do You Have the Aptitude & Personality to Be A Popular Author?

Professional Creative Writing Assessments

Anne Hart

ASJA Press

New York   Bloomington

iUniverse books may be ordered through booksellers or by contacting:

iUniverse
1663 Liberty Drive
Bloomington, IN 47403
www.iuniverse.com
1-800-Authors (1-800-288-4677)

ISBN: 978-1-4401-2520-1 (sc)

Printed in the United States of America

iUniverse rev. date: 03/05/2009

Table of Contents

PART I

Historical Fiction
Dénouement Creative Writing
Aptitude Classifier Quiz

Creative Writing Assessment

☙ *What really sells well currently in fiction?*

1. Eye-candy beginning that does not delay action.

2. Don't delay action by using a too-technical a description for average reader to follow in a romantic suspense novel. Example, you're writing about DNA researchers. Don't have the dialogue discuss too much technical material or try to explain it to the readers. Just use one short sentence in the dialogue per character to explain. Most agents reject too technical a novel.

3. Your synopsis should not repeat the story line. The story line needs to be clear in one or two short sentences. Most synopses rejected just keep repeating the same story line. Instead, you need to divulge the final denouement.

4. Commercially suitable work needs these three parts above plus a commercial title. For example instead of calling your DNA novel "The DNA Hunters" you can put it into the romantic intrigue genre by calling it The Bride Wore a Double Helix and then explain in ten plain language words what a double helix is all about.

☙ *Simple, Clear, and Universal*

Emphasize commitment rather than technical jargon. Make sure your fiction doesn't get too technical for the average reader, yet doesn't at the same time talk down to the average reader who could be anyone from a homemaker to a lawyer, nurse, professor, or physician writing mainstream, historical, romance, mystery, fantasy, science fiction, board or video games, or other genre novels, stories, plays, or scripts.

It's interesting that most agents don't want to handle novels that have too much technical information in them that is too much emphasis placed on scientific research in one's novel. Many agents and editors find that technical research results were "not interesting" (in their words).... but they didn't detail what "interesting" means to editors or agents. It all depends upon your intended audience. Ask yourself for whom you are writing.

Are you best-suited to be a historical novelist, mystery writer, short story sprinter, digital interactive story writer on ancient civilizations, a nonfiction writer, or an author of thrillers using historical settings or universal themes? Do you think like a fiction writer, investigative journalist, or an imaginative, creative nonfiction author writing biography in the style of genre or mainstream fiction?

How are you going to clarify and resolve the issues, problems, or situations in your plot by the way your characters behave to move the action forward? How do you get measurable results when writing fiction or creative nonfiction? Consider what steps you show to reveal how your story is resolved by the characters. This also is known as the d**énouement.**

Dénouement as it applies to a short story or novel is the final resolution. It's your clarification of a dramatic or narrative plot. What category of **dénouement** will your characters take to move the plot forward?

Take the writing style preference classifier and find out how you approach your favorite writing style using Toot's facts and acts. Which genre is for you--interactive, traditional, creative nonfiction, fiction, decisive or investigative?

Would you rather write for readers that need to interact with their own story endings or plot branches? Which style best fits you? What's your writing profile?

Enjoy this ancient echoes writing genre interest classifier and see the various ways in which way you can be more creative.

Do you prefer to write investigative, logical nonfiction or imaginative fiction—or a mixture of both? There are 35 questions—seven questions for each of the five pairs. There are 10 choices.

THE CHOICES:	
Grounded	Verve
Rational	Enthusiastic
Decisive	Investigative
Loner	Outgoing
Traditional	Change-Driven

Writer's Creativity Style, Personality, & Aptitude Assessment

Creative (imaginative) writing (fiction or nonfiction) is about building and being remembered for what you build into your story, fractal by fractal and word by word. Civilizations are remembered for either what they build up or what they tear down.

And your plot and story line can be the reason for their behaviors. Your characters can work for freedoms and equality for all, regardless of diversity, belief, or no belief, for unity, or for the right to remain nomadic or any other way you want them to be.

How do you want your story's characters and the plot (driven by characters) to be remembered by the world--by what they invent, create, or develop, or by what they implode, remove, or wipe out?

If a group of people are travelers or nomads, they can build stories from oral traditions out of seemingly "nothing" if the geographic areas they cover have no building materials such as trees or stone. Or art can be created on looms or from clay and minerals or from metals.

Creativity can be oral or artistic and can be told, recorded, or worn. You want your characters to be remembered for destroying a plague or disease or for building huge malls, enormous or useful architecture, or great centers of learning? Do you want your characters to be remembered for solving worldwide problems and getting measurable results? For providing detailed steps for others to follow? For moral and ethical revelations? Or as leaders and inventors? Or for taking humanity to newer planets? What is your goal as an imaginative writer? What are your preferences?

You are a historical **mystery writer** working on a novel, script, story, or an interactive audio book of adventure fiction with clues for the Web about a scribe in ancient Egypt, 1,350 B.C., who has unending adventures trying to track down the person who bashed King Toot with a golden vulture mallet and a cobra-headed hammer.

Your scribe is in a race against time to save Toot's teenaged widow, Ankh-Es-En-Amen, from being forced into an unwilling marriage with Toot's male nanny-Regent, Aye, who is determined to become Pharaoh by marrying the Queen. How will you write this interactive story, according to your writing style preferences?

✎ Clues

The leading character is 'Mose,' the scribe, not the prophet, Moses. The name Mose or Moses in ancient Egyptian means "from the water." The name "Toot Mose" means "wise one from the water" (The name usually means gift of the Nile.) Toot means wise and is represented in hieroglyphics as an owl.

Mose inherited wealth from an ancestral line of architects. He's an Egyptian male scribe, age 20, living in the royal palace. He grew up as Toot's friend. Called "Mu" for short, this character is your alter ego and takes on your own personality as he solves problems or crimes.

1. **To write your story, would you prefer to**

   a. go to the Hittite archives in order to have translated two letters sent by Toot's teenage widow to the Hittite king asking to send her a new husband (down-to-earth) **or**

   b. dig deeper and find out the connections between the two documents, reading fear between the lines and noting the reluctance Toot's widow expresses in being forced to marry her servant, the Regent Aye? (verve)

      a. □

      b. □

2. **Would you be more interested in researching history and writing about**

   a. the closeness of the relationship that surfaced between the Hittites and the Egyptians in 1,350 BCE (enthusiastic) **or**

   b. analyze the business deals and diplomatic events between these equal powers to see who was winning the race to becoming the superpower of the century? (rational)

      a. ☐

      b. ☐

3. **Are you more interested in the fact that**

   a. Toot's queen wrote all her letters in a Hittite dialect, not in Egyptian (down-to-earth) **or**

   b. King Toot's father, Akhenaten, was so hated after his death because he worshipped one deity, that his face was scratched off all his monuments and wall friezes? (verve)

      a. ☐

      b. ☐

4. **Would you rather write about**

   a. Toot being adopted, sent as a gift from Hatti during his Egyptian step father's "durbar" festival of his 12th year of reign (enthusiastic) **or**

   b. the mystery of why Toot was buried with both the Hittite vulture on his head and an Egyptian cobra on his crown? (rational)?

a. ☐

b. ☐

5. You are Toot's Queen. Would you rather

a. exercise your right as a widow to claim Toot's unmarried Hittite brother, Prince Zennanza (enthusiastic) **or**

b. marry Toot's male nanny because it's only right and fair to restore an Egyptian to Egypt's throne? (rational)

a. ☐

b. ☐

6. Toot's widow wrote to her father-in-law to send her another of his sons for marriage to her. As a writer of her life story, would you rather

a. create a laundry list of princes that she must interview and screen in a dating game (down-to-earth) **or**

b. create a story where she rides 1,000 miles on a donkey to run away from her servant after he forces her to marry him and has magical adventures disguised as a 14-year old boy studying philosophy and alchemy with Babylonian astrologers? (verve)

a. ☐

b. ☐

7. **Are you more interested in ending your story with**

   a. Aye marrying Toot's young widow, then taking Toot's adoptive grandmother, Queen Tiye as a second wife, so that you have closure and an ending for your story (decisive) **or**

   b. would you rather let your story remain open for serialization, since Toot's widow is never heard from again after Aye marries her and then marries Queen Tiye, since the fate of Toot's widow after marrying Aye is not recorded in history? (investigative)

      a. ☐

      b. ☐

8. **If you were prince Zennanza, would you prefer to**

   a. decide immediately to obey the Hittite King and leave your own country to marry the widowed Queen of Egypt because duty required it, knowing you'll probably be killed when you arrive by the same person who killed Toot, (decisive) **or**

   b. stall for time as long as possible, waiting for validated information to arrive regarding the diplomatic climate between Hittites and Egyptians? (investigative).

      a. ☐

      b. ☐

9. **You are King Toot, Pharaoh of Egypt, a Hittite prince adopted in infancy as a gift from the Hittite king because the Egyptian queen had six daughters. If you were King Toot, would you**

   a. speak in the Indo-European Hittite language in front of your Hamitic-speaking Egyptian Regent, thereby possibly inflaming the nationalism in him (investigative) or

   b. plan and organize methodically to have a whole line of people close to you from your own country of origin (in what is now called central Turkey) rather than from Egypt in which you were raised? (decisive)

   a. □

   b. □

10. **Would you rather write about**

   a. terms of the treaty between Hatti and Kemet (Egypt) based on the facts provided by records (down-to-earth) or

   b. the theories set in motion when Aye marries Toot's widow and soon after, the widow disappears, and Aye marries Queen Tiye? (verve)

   a. □

   b. □

11. Do you like writing about

a. enigmas or puzzles set in motion by symbols on intimate funerary equipment in a mystery novel (rational) **or**

b. why no other Egyptian royalty or deities after Toot's life span ever again were depicted with a vulture being friendly with a cobra? (enthusiastic)

    a. □

    b. □

12. A *tag line* shows the mood/emotion in the voice--*how* a character speaks or acts. Are you more interested in

a. compiling, counting, and indexing *citations* or *quotes* from how-to books for writers (down-to-earth) **or**

b. compiling *tag lines* that explain in fiction dialogue the specific behaviors or gestures such as, "Yes, he replied *timorously....*"? (verve)

    a. □

    b. □

13. Would you rather write

a. dialog (enthusiastic) **or**

b. description? (rational)

    a. □

    b. □

14. **To publicize your writing, would you rather**

   a. give spectacular presentations or shows without preparation or prior notice (investigative) or

   b. have to prepare a long time in advance to speak or perform? (decisive)

   a. ☐

   b. ☐

15. **If you were Queen Ankh-Es-En-Amen, would you prefer to**

   a. receive warnings well in advance and without surprises that Aye is planning to get rid of you and marry Queen Tiye (adoptive grandmother of Toot); so you could conveniently disappear (decisive) **or**

   b. adapt to last-moment changes by never getting down to your last man or your last beer? (investigative)

   a. ☐

   b. ☐

16. **As a scribe, artist, and poet in ancient Egypt would you**

   a. feel constrained by King Toot's time schedules and deadlines (due dates) (investigative) **or**

b. set realistic timetables and juggle priorities? (decisive)

a. □

b. □

17. As Toot's widow, do you feel bound to

a. go with social custom, do the activities itemized on the social calendar, and marry your dead husband's unmarried brother because it's organized according to a plan (decisive) **or**

b. go with the flow of the relationship, deal with issues as they arise, make no commitments or assumptions about what's the right thing to do because time changes plans? (investigative)

a. □

b. □

18. You're the Hittite King, Shup-Pilu-Liu-Mas reading Toot's widow's desperate letter in your own country. Is your reply to the Egyptian Queen more likely to be

a. one brief, concise, and to the point letter (rational) **or**

b. one sociable, friendly, empathetic and time-consuming letter? (enthusiastic)

a. □

b. □

19. You're King Toot contemplating who most wants to replace you with an Egyptian ruler. You make a list of

a. the pros and cons of each person close to you (rational) **or**

b. varied comments from friends and relatives on what they say behind your back regarding how your influence them and what they want from you. (enthusiastic)

a. ☐

b. ☐

20. You're the scribe trying to solve Toot's murder in ancient Egypt. Would you rather investigate

a. the tried and true facts about Aye (down-to-earth) **or**

b. want to see what's in the overall picture before you fill in the clues? (verve)

a. ☐

b. ☐

21. You're a scribe painting Toot's tomb shortly after his demise and you

a. seldom make errors of detail when looking for clues such as taking notice of Aye's wedding present to the young, healthy Queen--her freshly inscribed coffin. (down-to-earth) or

b. prefer more innovative work like writing

secret love poems to the Queen disguised as prayers and watching for Toot's ghost to escape through the eight-inch square hole cut in the rock of his tomb. (verve)

a. ☐

b. ☐

22. As a scribe in ancient Egypt, you become

a. tired when you work alone all day in a dimly torchlit tomb (outgoing) **or**

b. tired when King Toot interrupts your concentration on your work to demand that you greet and entertain his guests all evening at banquets. (loner).

    a. ☐

    b. ☐

23. When the Queen asks you as a scribe to write love poems for her that she can hand to Toot, you

a. create the ideas for your poems by long discussions with the Queen (outgoing) **or**

b. prefer to be alone when you reach deep down inside your spirit to listen to what your Ka and Ba (soul entities) tell you as the only resource for writing metaphors. (loner)

    a. ☐

    b. ☐

24. **You are in ancient Egypt investigating the death of Toot and prefer to**

a. question many different foreigners and locals at boisterous celebrations in different languages (outgoing) **or**

b. disregard outside events and look inside the family history/genealogy inscriptions on a *stellae* (stone tablet or obelisk) for the culprit. (loner)

   a. □

   b. □

25. **King Toot, at age nine asks you to develop ideas for him about how to act when ascending the throne so young. You prefer to develop ideas through**

a. reflection, meditation, and prayer (loner) **or**

b. discussions and interviews among Toot's playmates on what makes Toot laugh. (outgoing)

   a. □

   b. □

26. **As a scribe you are**

a. rarely cautious about the family position of those with whom you socialize as long as they are kind, righteous people who do good deeds (outgoing) **or**

b. seeking one person with power to raise

you from scribe to governor of Egypt, if only the pharaoh would ask your advice. (loner)

a. ☐

b. ☐

27. **You are a sculptor in ancient Egypt when the pharaoh asks you to carve a name for yourself on a marble column that's a special representation of its owner. Would you**

a. inscribe the hieroglyph that means 'remote' (loner) or

b. choose a special name for yourself that means, "He who shares time easily with many foreigners?" (outgoing)

    a. ☐

    b. ☐

28. **As an ancient scribe, do you work better when you**

a. spend your day off where no one can see you asking the Sphinx why its claws are so sharp and made of reef-formed limestone (loner) **or**

b. spend your free time training teams of apprentice scribes to sculpt their own faces? (outgoing)

    a. ☐

    b. ☐

29. If you discovered a new land, would you build your cities upon

a. your wise elders' principles as they always have worked well before (traditional) **or**

b. unfamiliar cargo that traders brought from afar to civilize your land? (change-driven)

a.☐

b.☐

30. Do you depict your king's victories on a stone column exactly as

a. surviving witnesses from both sides recounted the events (change-driven) or

b. the pharaoh wants people to see? (traditional)

a.☐

b.☐

31. If you're self-motivated, would you avoid learning from your overseer because

a. your overseer doesn't keep up with the times (change-driven) **or**

b. your overseer doesn't let you follow in your father's footsteps? (traditional)

a.☐

b.☐

32. Would you prefer to

a. train scribes because your father taught you how to do it well (traditional) **or**

b. move quickly from one project to another forever? (change-driven)

   a.☐

   b.☐

33. Do you feel like an outsider when

a. you think more about the future than about current chores (change-driven) **or**

b. invaders replace your forefathers' familiar foods with unfamiliar cuisine? (traditional)

   a.☐

   b.☐

34. Do you quickly

a. solve problems for those inside when you're coming from outside (change-driven) **or**

b. refuse to spend your treasures to develop new ideas that might fail? (traditional)

   a.☐

   b.☐

35. Would you rather listen to and learn from philosophers that

a. predict a future in which old habits are replaced with new ones (change-driven) **or**

b. are only interested in experiencing one day at a time? (traditional)

a.☐

b.☐

Self-Scoring the Test

Add up the number of answers for each of the following ten writing style traits for the 35 questions. There are seven questions for each group. The ten categories are made up of five opposite pairs.

Down-to-earth	Verve
Rational	Enthusiastic
Decisive	Investigative
Loner	Outgoing
Traditional	Change-Driven

Then put the numbers for each answer next to the categories. See the same self-scored test and results below.

1. Total Down-to-earth
2. Total Rational
3. Total Decisive
4. Total Loner
5. Total Traditional

6. Total Verve
7. Total Enthusiastic
8. Total Investigative
9. Total Outgoing
10. Total Change-Driven

To get your score, you're only adding up the number of answers for each of the 10 categories (five pairs) above. See the sample self-scored test below. Note that there are seven questions for each of the five pairs (or 10 designations). There are 35 questions. Seven questions times five categories equal 35 questions. Keep the number of questions you design for each category equal.

Sample Scored Test

⊷ Take the "King Toot" Creative Writing Aptitude Classifier Quiz

Are you best-suited to be a digital interactive story writer on ancient Egypt, a nonfiction writer, or a mystery writer using ancient Egyptian themes or related ancient themes? Do you think like a fiction writer? Take the writing style preference classifier and find out how you approach your favorite writing style using Toot's facts and acts.

Which genre is for you--interactive, traditional, creative nonfiction, fiction, decisive or investigative? Would you rather write for readers that need to interact with their own story endings or plot branches? Which style best fits you? What's your writing profile?

Take this ancient echoes writing genre interest classifier and see the various ways in which way you can be more creative. Do you prefer to write investigative, logical nonfiction or imaginative fiction—or a mixture of both?

⤙ *The 10 Choices:*

THE CHOICES:	
Grounded	Verve
Rational	Enthusiastic
Decisive	Investigative
Loner	Outgoing
Traditional	Change-Driven

Writer's Creativity Style Classifier

You are a **mystery writer** working on an interactive audio book for the Web about a scribe in ancient Egypt, 1,350 B.C., who has unending adventures trying to track down the person who bashed King Toot with a golden vulture mallet and a cobra-headed hammer.

Your scribe is in a race against time to save Toot's teenaged widow, Ankh-Es-En-Amen, from being forced into an unwilling marriage with Toot's male nanny-Regent, Aye, who is determined to become Pharaoh by marrying the Queen. How will you write this interactive story, according to your writing style preferences?

↞ *Clues*

The leading character is 'Mose,' the scribe, not the prophet, Moses. The name Mose or Moses in ancient Egyptian means "from the water." The name "Toot Mose" means "wise one from the water" (The name usually means gift of the Nile.) Toot means wise and is represented in hieroglyphics as an owl.

Mose inherited wealth from an ancestral line of architects. He's an Egyptian male scribe, age 20, living in the royal palace. He grew up as Toot's friend. Called "Mu" for short, this character is your alter ego and takes on your own personality as he solves problems or crimes.

1. **To write your story, would you prefer to**

    a. go to the Hittite archives in order to have translated two letters sent by Toot's teenage widow to the Hittite king asking to send her a new husband (down-to-earth) **or**

    b. dig deeper and find out the connections between the two documents, reading fear between the lines and noting the reluctance Toot's widow expresses in being forced to marry her servant, the Regent Aye? (verve)

    a. □

    b. ■

2. **Would you be more interested in research-ing history and writing about**

    a. the closeness of the relationship that sur-faced between the Hittites and the Egyp-tians in 1,350 BCE (enthusiastic) **or**

    b. analyze the business deals and diplomatic events between these equal powers to see who was winning the race to becoming the superpower of the century? (rational)

        a. ■

        b. □

3. **Are you more interested in the fact that**

    a. Toot's queen wrote all her letters in a Hit-tite dialect, not in Egyptian (down-to-earth) **or**

    b. King Toot's father, Akhenaten, was so hat-ed after his death because he worshipped one deity, that his face was scratched off all his monuments and wall friezes? (verve)

        a. □

        b. ■

4. **Would you rather write about**

    a. Toot being adopted, sent as a gift from Hatti during his Egyptian step father's "durbar" festival of his 12th year of reign (enthusiastic) **or**

    b. the mystery of why Toot was buried with both the Hittite vulture on his head and an Egyptian cobra on his crown? (rational)?

a. ■

b. □

5. **You are Toot's Queen. Would you rather**

a. exercise your right as a widow to claim Toot's unmarried Hittite brother, Prince Zennanza (enthusiastic) **or**

b. marry Toot's male nanny because it's only right and fair to restore an Egyptian to Egypt's throne? (rational)

    a. ■

    b. □

6. **Toot's widow wrote to her father-in-law to send her another of his sons for marriage to her. As a writer of her life story, would you rather**

a. create a laundry list of princes that she must interview and screen in a dating game (down-to-earth) **or**

b. create a story where she rides 1,000 miles on a donkey to run away from her servant after he forces her to marry him and has magical adventures disguised as a 14-year old boy studying philosophy and alchemy with Babylonian astrologers? (verve)

    a. □

    b. ■

7. **Are you more interested in ending your story with**

   a. Aye marrying Toot's young widow, then taking Toot's adoptive grandmother, Queen Tiye as a second wife, so that you have closure and an ending for your story (decisive) **or**

   b. would you rather let your story remain open for serialization, since Toot's widow is never heard from again after Aye marries her and then marries Queen Tiye, since the fate of Toot's widow after marrying Aye is not recorded in history? (investigative)

      a. □

      b. ■

8. **If you were prince Zennanza, would you prefer to**

   a. decide immediately to obey the Hittite King and leave your own country to marry the widowed Queen of Egypt because duty required it, knowing you'll probably be killed when you arrive by the same person who killed Toot, (decisive) **or**

   b. stall for time as long as possible, waiting for validated information to arrive regarding the diplomatic climate between Hittites and Egyptians? (investigative).

      a. □

b. ■

9. **You are King Toot, Pharaoh of Egypt, a Hittite prince adopted in infancy as a gift from the Hittite king because the Egyptian queen had six daughters. If you were King Toot, would you**

   a. speak in the Indo-European Hittite language in front of your Hamitic-speaking Egyptian Regent, thereby possibly inflaming the nationalism in him (investigative) **or**

   b. plan and organize methodically to have a whole line of people close to you from your own country of origin (in what is now called central Turkey) rather than from Egypt in which you were raised? (decisive)

      a. ■
      b. □

10. **Would you rather write about**

    a. terms of the treaty between Hatti and Kemet (Egypt) based on the facts provided by records (down-to-earth) or

    b. the theories set in motion when Aye marries Toot's widow and soon after, the widow disappears, and Aye marries Queen Tiye? (verve)

       a. □
       b. ■

11. Do you like writing about

a. enigmas or puzzles set in motion by symbols on intimate funerary equipment in a mystery novel (rational) **or**

b. why no other Egyptian royalty or deities after Toot's life span ever again were depicted with a vulture being friendly with a cobra? (enthusiastic)

   a. ☐

   b. ■

12. A *tag line* shows the mood/emotion in the voice--how a character speaks or acts. Are you more interested in

a. compiling, counting, and indexing *citations* or *quotes* from how-to books for writers (down-to-earth) or

b. compiling *tag lines* that explain in fiction dialogue the specific behaviors or gestures such as, "Yes, he replied timorously."? (verve)

   a. ☐

   b. ■

13. Would you rather write

a. dialog (enthusiastic) **or**

b. description? (rational)

   a. ■

   b. ☐

14. To publicize your writing, would you rather

a. give spectacular presentations or shows without preparation or prior notice (investigative) **or**

b. have to prepare a long time in advance to speak or perform? (decisive)

    a. ■

    b. □

15. If you were Queen Ankh-Es-En-Amen, would you prefer to

a. receive warnings well in advance and without surprises that Aye is planning to get rid of you and marry Queen Tiye (adoptive grandmother of Toot); so you could conveniently disappear (decisive) **or**

b. adapt to last-moment changes by never getting down to your last man or your last beer? (investigative)

    a. □

    b. ■

16. As a scribe, artist, and poet in ancient Egypt would you

a. feel constrained by King Toot's time schedules and deadlines (due dates) (investigative) or

b. set realistic timetables and juggle priorities? (decisive)

a. ■

b. □

17. As Toot's widow, do you feel bound to

a. go with social custom, do the activities itemized on the social calendar, and marry your dead husband's unmarried brother because it's organized according to a plan (decisive) or

b. go with the flow of the relationship, deal with issues as they arise, make no commitments or assumptions about what's the right thing to do because time changes plans? (investigative)

a. □

b. ■

18. You're the Hittite King, Shup-Pilu-Liu-Mas reading Toot's widow's desperate letter in your own country. Is your reply to the Egyptian Queen more likely to be

a. one brief, concise, and to the point letter (rational) **or**

b. one sociable, friendly, empathetic and time-consuming letter? (enthusiastic)

a. □

b. ■

19. **You're King Toot contemplating who most wants to replace you with an Egyptian ruler. You make a list of**

a. the pros and cons of each person close to you (rational) **or**

b. varied comments from friends and relatives on what they say behind your back regarding how your influence them and what they want from you. (enthusiastic)

   a. ☐

   b. ■

20. **You're the scribe trying to solve Toot's murder in ancient Egypt. Would you rather investigate**

a. the tried and true facts about Aye (down-to-earth) **or**

b. want to see what falls under the all-inclusive umbrella before you fill in the clues? (verve)

   a. ☐

   b. ■

21. **You're a scribe painting Toot's tomb shortly after his demise and you**

a. seldom make errors of detail when looking for clues such as taking notice of Aye's wedding present to the young, healthy Queen--her freshly inscribed coffin. (down-to-earth) **or**

b. prefer more innovative work like writing secret love poems to the Queen disguised as prayers and watching for Toot's ghost to escape through the eight-inch square hole cut in the rock of his tomb. (verve)

a. □

b. ■

22. As a scribe in ancient Egypt, you become

a. tired when you work alone all day in a dimly torchlit tomb (outgoing) **or**

b. tired when King Toot interrupts your concentration on your work to demand that you greet and entertain his guests all evening at banquets. (loner).

a. □

b. ■

23. When the Queen asks you as a scribe to write love poems for her that she can hand to Toot, you

a. create the ideas for your poems by long discussions with the Queen (outgoing) or

b. prefer to be alone when you reach deep down inside your spirit to listen to what your Ka and Ba (soul entities) tell you as the only resource for writing metaphors. (loner)

a. □

b. ■

24. **You are in ancient Egypt investigating the death of Toot and prefer to**

a. question many different foreigners and locals at boisterous celebrations in different languages (outgoing) **or**

b. disregard outside events and look inside the family history/genealogy inscriptions on a stellae for the culprit. (loner)

    a. ☐

    b. ■

25. **King Toot, at age nine asks you to develop ideas for him about how to act when ascending the throne so young. You prefer to develop ideas through**

a. reflection, meditation, and prayer (loner) **or**

b. discussions and interviews among Toot's playmates on what makes Toot laugh. (outgoing)

    a. ☐

    b. ■

26. **As a scribe you are**

a. rarely cautious about the family position of those with whom you socialize as long as they are kind, righteous people who do good deeds (outgoing) **or**

b. seeking one person with power to raise you from scribe to governor of Egypt, if only the pharaoh would ask your advice. (loner)

a. ■

b. □

27. You are a sculptor in ancient Egypt when the pharaoh asks you to carve a name for yourself on a marble column that's a special representation of its owner. Would you

a. inscribe the hieroglyph that means 'remote' (loner) **or**

b. choose a special name for yourself that means, "He who shares time easily with many foreigners?" (outgoing)

    a. □

    b. ■

28. As an ancient scribe, do you work better when you

a. spend your day off where no one can see you asking the Sphinx why its claws are so sharp and made of reef-formed limestone (loner) **or**

b. spend your free time training teams of apprentice scribes to sculpt their own faces? (outgoing)

    a. ■

    b. □

29. If you discovered a new land, would you build your cities upon

a. your wise elders' principles as they always have worked well before (traditional) or

b. unfamiliar cargo that traders brought from afar to civilize your land? (change-driven)

    a. □

    b. ■

30. Do you depict your king's victories on a stone column exactly as

a. surviving witnesses from both sides recounted the events (change-driven) **or**

b. the pharaoh wants people to see? (traditional)

    a.□

    b.■

31. If you're self-motivated, would you avoid learning from your overseer because

a. your overseer doesn't keep up with the times (change-driven) **or**

b. your overseer doesn't let you follow in your father's footsteps? (traditional)

    a. ■

    b. □

32. Would you prefer to

    a. train scribes because your father taught you how to do it well (traditional) or

    b. move quickly from one project to another forever? (change-driven)

      a. □

      b. ■

33. Do you feel like an outsider when

    a. you think more about the future than about current chores (change-driven) **or**

    b. invaders replace your forefathers' familiar foods with unfamiliar cuisine? (traditional)

      a. ■

      b. □

34. Do you quickly

    a. solve problems for those inside when you're coming from outside (change-driven) or

    b. refuse to spend your treasures to develop new ideas that might fail? (traditional)

      a. ■

      b. □

35. Would you rather listen to and learn from philosophers that

    a. predict a future in which old habits are replaced with new ones (change-driven) or

b. are only interested in experiencing one day at a time? (traditional)

a. □

b. ■

Scores

Total Down-to-earth	0	Total Verve	5
Total Rational	0	Total Enthusiastic	7
Total Decisive	0	Total Investigative	7
Total Loner	4	Total Outgoing	3
Total Traditional	2	Total Change-Driven	5

The four highest numbers of answers are enthusiastic, investigative, imaginative loner. Choose the highest numbers first as having the most importance (or weight) in your writing style preference. Therefore, your own *creative writing **style*** *and the way you plot your character's actions, interests, and goals* (for fiction writing and specifically mystery writing) is an ***enthusiastic investigative vivacious (verve-with-imagination) loner***. Your five personality letters would be: E I V L C. (Scramble the letters to make a word to remember, the name Clive, in this case.)

Note that there is a tie between C and V. Both have a score of '5'. However, since 'V' (verve) which signifies vivacious imagination with gusto competes with 'C', being change-driven, the 'verve' in the vivacious personality wracked with creative imagination would wither in a traditional corporation that emphasizes routinely running a tight ship. Traditional firms seek to imitate successful corporations of the past that worked well and still work. They don't need to be fixed often unless they make noise.

Instead, the dominantly change-driven creative individual would flourish better with a forward-looking, trend-setting creative corporation and build security from flexibility of job skill. When in doubt, turn to action verbs to communicate your 'drive.' If you're misplaced, you won't connect as well with co-workers and may be dubbed "a loose cannon."

You know you're writing in the right genre when your personality connects with the genre of fiction or creative nonfiction readers and groups to share meaning. Communication is the best indicator of your personality matching a novel's main character traits with readers. It's all about connecting more easily with readers similar to your preferences.

Your main character or alter-ego could probably be an enthusiastic investigative imaginative loner. But you'd not only have lots of imagination and creativity—but also verve, that vivacious gusto. You'd have fervor, dash, and élan.

The easily excitable, investigative, creative/imaginative loner described as having verve, is more likely to represent what you feel inside your core personality, your self-insight, as you explore your own values and interests.

It's what you feel like, what your *values* represent on this test at this moment in time. That's how a lot of personality tests work. This one is customized for fiction writers. Another test could be tailored for career area interests or for analyzing what stresses you. Think of your personality as your virtues.

Qualities on this customized test that are inherent in the test taker who projects his or her values and personality traits onto the characters would represent more of a sentimental, charismatic, imaginative, investigative individual who likes to work alone most of the time.

The person could at times be more change-driven than traditional. The real test is whether the test taker is consistent about these traits or values on many different assessments of interests, personality, or values.

What's being tested here is imaginative fiction writing style. Writing has a personality, genre, or character of its own. The writing style and values are revealed in the way the characters drive the plot.

These sample test scores measure the preference, interest, and trait of the writer. The tone and mood are measured in this test. It's a way of sharing meaning, of communicating by driving the characters and the plot in a selected direction.

This assessment 'score' reveals a fiction writer who is enthusiastically investigative in tone, mood, and texture. These 'traits' or values apply to the writer as well as to the primary characters in the story.

The traits driving a writer's creativity also drive the main characters. Writer and characters work in a partnership of alter egos to move the plot forward. A creativity test lets you select and express the action, attitudes, and values of the story in a world that you shape according to clues, critical thinking, and personal likes.

PART II

Anne Hart's
Professional Creative
Non Fiction Writer's
Job Task Interest Classifier

The classifier consists of *twenty-eight questions* that are designed to measure your preferred *style* of full-time professional creative **nonfiction** writing (*including creative nonfiction and memoirs*) and communication/connection clarity that forges positive attitudes in editorial work for all types of communicators such as the following:

> *journalists,*
>
> *technical and medical writers,*
>
> *various science writers such as nutrition journalists*
>
> *creative genealogy and DNA-driven genealogy journalists*
>
> *family and personal history writers/producers/biographers*
>
> *oral historians*
>
> *general assignment editors and journalists*
>
> *technical/medical indexers*
>
> *publicists and communications-related educators*
>
> *corporate report and marketing writers*
>
> *case history success story managers*
>
> *human resources editors and career development writers researchers*
>
> *creative nonfiction writing educators, writing teachers,*
>
> *and public/professional speakers with books or videos.*

tions, transfer your page totals to the score sheet. Have fun. Enjoy the assessment.

1. **You would rather promote your latest book by:**

   a. An author tour. ☐

   b. Online chats. ☐

2. **Where will your research start for your next article or book?**

   a. Interviewing out in the field. ☐

   b. Recording your inner hunch. ☐

3. **Most of your ideas for writing reflect:**

   a. Your internal feelings or thoughts. ☐

   b. Current issues in the news about people. ☐

4. **What kind of relationship would you like with your publisher?**

   a. Direct contact by phone. ☐

   b. Indirect contact via email. ☐

5. **How do you feel after conducting an interview?**

   a. Energized enough to open more doors. ☐

b. Exhausted enough to
meditate in seclusion. □

6. **Which article interests you enough to re-search?**

   a. A question-and-answer interview. □

   b. A collection of one-line quotes.   □

7. **Which work style would interest you most?**

   a. Collaboration with team
   mates over lunch. □

   b. Working alone on a book
   at your own pace. □

8. **In investigating and reporting crime news, which set of clues would you prefer to finally expose the culprit?**

   a. Dates and facts on the culprit's letters. □

   b. Your own inner hunch about
   the culprit's personality. □

9. **Would you rather write:**

   a. Practical-how-to articles or books? □

   b. Books or reports that forecast trends? □

10. **Which company feels like the best-fit work place?**

    a. A traditional periodical
    with a fact-checker. □

b.   A socially bold venture capitalist pushing the limits. □

11. If you were an editor-in-chief, which job would you want to?

a.   Edit a trendy fashion, sports, or travel magazine. □

b.   Edit industrial, government, or technical trade journals. □

12. When writing professionally, would you rather:

a.   Keep sentences under ten words with bulleted lists? □

b.   Use metaphors and mind-mapping visuals? □

13. You most often write about:

a.   The process. □

b.   The result. □

14. Which would you rather review?

a.   A textbook, guidebook, or manual. □

b.   A novel. □

15. How do you decide?

a.   By reasoning, thinking, or logic. □

b.   By gut hunches. □

16. Which topic would most interest you?

a.   Entertainment law. ☐

b.   Storytelling. ☐

17. Would you rather see your byline on?

a.   Amazing True Life Story
      Confessions Magazine. ☐

b.   Rough Terrain Wheelchair
      Technology Design Magazine. ☐

18. Would you rather write or edit for a publisher who:

a.   Outsmarts the competition
      with 10 proven tactics? ☐

b.   Cultivates creative expression
      brainstorming lunches? ☐

19. Would you rather write about?

a.   New applications of artificial
      intelligence and heuristics. ☐

b.   Virtual reality therapy
      for agoraphobia. ☐

20. Which topic would you rather investigate as your new hobby?

a.   Niche or ethnic romance online. ☐

b.   Robots, avatars, and smart
      agents online. ☐

Circle the letter under your highest score in each category. Then write the circle's letter in the corresponding blank spaces below to reveal your personality preference.

Congratulations! You're an ___ ___ ___ ___ ___
                            I II III IV V

PART III

Take the "Howling Wolf's Scribe"* Creative Writing Preference Classifier

©2007 by Anne Hart

---

*   Also see my ***Howling Wolf Scribe*** fiction writer's creativity enhancement assessment (for entertainment purposes) in print in my paperback book titled, 30+ Brain-Exercising Creativity Coach Businesses to Open: How to Use Writing, Music, Drama & Art Therapy Techniques for Healing copyright by Anne Hart, M.A. ISBN-13: 978-0-595-42710-9. Published by ASJA Press imprint, iUniverse, inc. 2007. (http://www.iuniverse.com). Click on Bookstore. Search paperback books by title.

Are you best-suited to be an ethnographic story writer, a nonfiction writer, digital interactive author, theatrical, cinematic, or a mystery writer using historic, imaginative, fantasy, and/or ethnographic themes? How about investigative journalism based on history or fiction based on historical themes? Do you think like a fiction writer? Take the writing style preference classifier and find out how you approach your favorite writing style using Zabeyko's facts and acts.

Which genre is for you--interactive, traditional, creative nonfiction, fiction, decisive or investigative? Would you rather write for readers that need to interact with their own story endings or plot branches? Which style best fits you? What's your writing profile?

Take this ancient echoes writing genre interest classifier and see the various ways in which way you can be more creative. Do you prefer to write investigative, logical nonfiction or imaginative fiction—or a mixture of both? There are 35 questions—seven questions for each of the five pairs. ***There are 10 choices.***

THE CHOICES:	
Grounded	Verve
Rational	Enthusiastic
Decisive	Investigative
Loner	Outgoing
Traditional	Change-Driven

b. tired when Zabeyko interrupts your concentration on your work to demand that you greet and entertain his guests all evening at banquets. (loner).

    a. ☐

    b. ☐

23. **When Jadwiga asks you as a scribe to write love poems for her that she can send to Zabeyko, you**

a. create the ideas for your poems by long discussions with her (outgoing) **or**

b. prefer to be alone when you reach deep down inside your spirit to listen to what your soul entities tell you as the only resource for writing metaphors. (loner)

    a. ☐

    b. ☐

24. **You travel to Venice and Vienna investigating the death of Zabeyko and prefer to**

a. question many different foreigners and locals at boisterous celebrations in different languages (outgoing) **or**

b. disregard outside events and look inside the family history/genealogy inscriptions for the culprit. (loner)

    a. ☐

    b. ☐

25. Zabeyko, at age nine asks you to develop ideas for him about how to act when writing music. You prefer to develop ideas through

a. reflection, meditation, and prayer (loner)**or**

b. discussions and interviews among Zabeyko's playmates on what makes Zabeyko laugh. (outgoing)

    a. □

    b. □

26. As a scribe you are

a. rarely cautious about the family position of those with whom you socialize as long as they are kind, righteous people who do good deeds (outgoing) **or**

b. seeking one person with power to raise you from scribe to noble, if only the richest noble in Wolkowysk would ask your advice. (loner)

    a. □

    b. □

27. You are a designer and builder of palaces. A rich noble asks you to carve a name for yourself on his palace door that's a special representation of its builder. Would you

a. inscribe the word that means 'remote' (loner) **or**

b. choose a special name for yourself that means, "He who shares time easily with many foreigners?" (outgoing)

a. ☐

b. ☐

28. As an early 19th century scribe, do you work better when you

a. spend your day off daydreaming where no one can see you (loner) **or**

b. spend your free time training teams of apprentice scribes? (outgoing)

a. ☐

b. ☐

29. If you discovered a new land, would you build your cities upon

a. your wise elders' principles as they always have worked well before (traditional) **or**

b. unfamiliar cargo that traders brought from afar? (change-driven)

a.☐

b.☐

30. Do you depict your ruler's victories on a stone column exactly as

a. surviving witnesses from both sides recounted the events (change-driven) **or**

b. only the ruler wants people to see? (traditional)

a.□

b.□

31. If you're self-motivated, would you avoid learning from your overseer because

a. your overseer doesn't keep up with the times (change-driven) **or**

b. your overseer doesn't let you follow in your father's footsteps? (traditional)

a.□

b.□

32. Would you prefer to

a. train the trainers because your father taught you how to do it well (traditional) **or**

b. move quickly from one project to another forever? (change-driven)

a.□

b.□

Here is a Sample Self-Scored Assessment with Answers

↬ Take the "Howling Wolf's Scribe" Creative Writing Preference Classifier ©2007 by Anne Hart

Are you best-suited to be a digital interactive or ethnographic story writer, a nonfiction writer, or a mystery writer using historic themes? Do you think like a fiction writer? Take the writing style preference classifier and find out how you approach your favorite writing style using Zabeyko's facts and acts.

Which genre is for you--interactive, traditional, creative nonfiction, fiction, decisive or investigative? Would you rather write for readers that need to interact with their own story endings or plot branches? Which style best fits you? What's your writing profile?

Take this ancient echoes writing genre interest classifier and see the various ways in which way you can be more creative. Do you prefer to write investigative, logical nonfiction or imaginative fiction—or a mixture of both? There are 35 questions—seven questions for each of the five pairs. There are 10 choices.

↬ The 10 Choices:

THE CHOICES:	
Grounded	Verve
Rational	Enthusiastic
Decisive	Investigative

Loner	Outgoing
Traditional	Change-Driven

Sample Scores

Total Down-to-earth	0	Total Verve	5
Total Rational	0	Total Enthusiastic	7
Total Decisive	0	Total Investigative	7
Total Loner	4	Total Outgoing	3
Total Traditional	2	Total Change-Driven	5

In the already self-scored sample assessment that follows, the four highest numbers of answers are enthusiastic, investigative, imaginative loner. Choose the highest numbers first as having the most importance (or weight) in your writing style preference.

Therefore, your own *creative writing* **style** *and the way you plot your character's actions, interests, and goals* (for fiction writing and specifically mystery writing) is an ***enthusiastic investigative vivacious (verve-with-imagination) loner***. **Your five personality letters would be: E I V L C.** (Scramble the letters to make a word to remember, the name Clive, in this case.)

Note that there is a tie between C and V. Both have a score of '5'. However, since 'V' (verve) which signifies vivacious imagination with gusto competes with 'C' being change-driven, the 'verve' in the vivacious personality wracked with creative imagination would wither in a traditional corporation that emphasizes routinely running a tight ship. Traditional firms seek to imitate successful corporations of the past that worked well and still work. They don't need to be fixed often unless they make noise.

Instead, the dominantly change-driven creative individual would flourish better with a forward-looking, trend-setting creative corporation and build security from flexibility of job skill. When in doubt, turn to action verbs to communicate your 'drive.' If you're misplaced, you won't connect as well with co-workers and may be dubbed "a loose cannon."

You know you're in the right job when your personality connects with the group to share meaning. Communication is the best indicator of your personality matching a corporation's character traits. It's all about connecting more easily.

Your main character or alter-ego could probably be an enthusiastic investigative imaginative loner. But you'd not only have lots of imagination and creativity—but also verve, that vivacious gusto. You'd have fervor, dash, and élan.

The easily excitable, investigative, creative/imaginative loner described as having verve, is more likely to represent what you feel inside your core personality, your self-insight, as you explore your own values and interests.

It's what you feel like, what your *values* represent on this test at this moment in time. That's how a lot of personality tests work. This one is customized for fiction writers. Another test could be tailored for career area interests or for analyzing what stresses you. Think of your personality as your virtues.

Qualities on this customized test that are inherent in the test taker who projects his or her values and personality traits onto the characters would represent more of a sentimental, charismatic, imaginative, investigative individual who likes to work alone most of the time.

The person could at times be more change-driven than traditional. The real test is whether the test taker is consistent about these traits or values on many different assessments of interests, personality, or values.

What's being tested here is imaginative fiction writing style. Writing has a personality, genre, or character of its own. The writing style and values are revealed in the way the characters drive the plot.

These sample test scores measure the preference, interest, and trait of the writer. The tone and mood are measured in this test. It's a way of sharing meaning, of communicating by driving the characters and the plot in a selected direction.

This assessment 'score' reveals a fiction writer who is enthusiastically investigative in tone, mood, and texture. These 'traits' or values apply to the writer as well as to the primary characters in the story.

The traits driving a writer's creativity also drive the main characters. Writer and characters work in a partnership of alter egos to move the plot forward. A creativity test lets you select and express the action, attitudes, and values of the story in a world that you shape according to clues, critical thinking, and personal likes. Below you'll see the definitions of the 10 key word choices in this assessment followed by the sample assessment that already is self-scored.

the Silk Road to study architecture where she meets her true soul mate and business partner. (verve)

a. □

b. ■

7. **Are you more interested in ending your story with**

a. Jagello marrying Zabeyko's fiancée, Jadwiga, then quickly getting rid of Jadwiga as Jagello marries Zabeyko's adoptive grandmother, Pradislava, for her land and property.as his second wife, so that you have closure and an ending for your story (decisive) **or**

b. would you rather let your story remain open for serialization, since Zabeyko's fiancée is never heard from again and disappears just like Zabeyko did after Jagello marries her and then marries his adoptive grandmother, Pradislava. The fate of Zabeyko's fiancée after marrying Zabeyko's tutor, Jagello is not recorded in history. (investigative)

a. □

b. ■

8. **If you were a Tatar prince living in a for-eign land, would you prefer to**

   a. decide immediately to obey the diverse European nobles of Wolkowysk and leave Tataristan to marry Jadwiga of the howl-ing wolf forests because duty required it, knowing you'll probably be killed when you arrive by the same person who killed Zabeyko, (decisive) **or**

   b. stall for time as long as possible, waiting for validated information to arrive regard-ing the diplomatic climate between Tatars and Russians? (investigative).

      a. ☐
      b. ■

9. **You are Zabeyko, a Tatar prince adopted in infancy by a wealthy Belarus owner of many traveling circus acts. You have been given as a gift from the Tatar king to the Baltic Tribes because his wife had six daughters and no sons. If you were Zabeyko, would you**

   a. speak in the Tatar tongue in front of your Slavic tutor, thereby possibly in-flaming the nationalism in him (inves-tigative) **or**

b. plan and organize methodically to have a whole line of people close to you from your own Tataristan rather than from the Slavic lands in which you were raised? (decisive)

    a. ■

    b. □

10. Would you rather write about

a. terms of the treaty between Tatars and the Slavs based on the facts provided by records (down-to-earth) **or**

b. the theories set in motion when Jagello marries Jadwiga and soon after, she disappears, just like her financee, Zabeyko, and Jabello then marries Zabeyko's mother? (verve)

    a. □

    b. ■

11. Do you like writing about

a. enigmas or puzzles set in motion by symbols on intimate funerary equipment in a mystery novel (rational) **or**

b. why no other Tatar royalty emblem after Zabeyko's life span ever again appeared on a medallion with a horse tamga inscribed in scrimshaw ivory with a vulture? (enthusiastic)

    a. □

    b. ■

12. A *tag line* shows the mood/emotion in the voice--how a character speaks or acts. Are you more interested in

a. compiling, counting, and indexing *citations* or *quotes* from how-to books for writers (down-to-earth) **or**

b. compiling *tag lines* that *explain* in fiction dialogue the specific behaviors or *gestures and body language* such as, "Yes," he replied timorously. (verve)

  a. □

  b. ■

13. Would you rather write

a. dialog (enthusiastic) or

b. description? (rational)

  a. ■

  b. □

14. To publicize your writing, would you rather

a. give spectacular presentations or shows without preparation or prior notice (investigative) **or**

b. have to prepare a long time in advance to speak or perform? (decisive)

  a. ■

  b. □

25. Zabeyko, at age nine asks you to develop ideas for him about how to act when writing music. You prefer to develop ideas through

a. reflection, meditation, and prayer (loner) **or**

b. discussions and interviews among Zabeyko's playmates on what makes Zabeyko laugh. (outgoing)

    a. □

    b. ■

26. As a scribe you are

a. rarely cautious about the family position of those with whom you socialize as long as they are kind, righteous people who do good deeds (outgoing) **or**

b. seeking one person with power to raise you from scribe to noble, if only the richest noble in Wolkowysk would ask your advice. (loner)

    a. ■

    b. □

27. You are a designer and builder of palaces. A rich noble asks you to carve a name for yourself on his palace door that's a special representation of its builder. Would you

a. inscribe the word that means 'remote' (loner) **or**

b. choose a special name for yourself that means, "He who shares time easily with many foreigners?" (outgoing)

a. ☐

b. ■

28. As an early 19th century scribe, do you work better when you

a. spend your day off daydreaming where no one can see you (loner) **or**

b. spend your free time training teams of apprentice scribes? (outgoing)

a. ■

b. ☐

29. If you discovered a new land, would you build your cities upon

a. your wise elders' principles as they always have worked well before (traditional) or

b. unfamiliar cargo that traders brought from afar? (change-driven)

a. ☐

b. ■

30. Do you depict your ruler's victories on a stone column exactly as

a. surviving witnesses from both sides recounted the events (change-driven) **or**

b. only the ruler wants people to see? (traditional)

    a.□

    b.■

31. If you're self-motivated, would you avoid learning from your overseer because

a. your overseer doesn't keep up with the times (change-driven) **or**

b. your overseer doesn't let you follow in your father's footsteps? (traditional)

    a. ■

    b. □

32. Would you prefer to

a. train the trainers because your father taught you how to do it well (traditional) **or**

b. move quickly from one project to another forever? (change-driven)

    a.□

    b. ■

33. Do you feel like an outsider when

a. you think more about future chores (change-driven) **or**

b. invaders replace your forefathers' familiar foods with unfamiliar cuisine? (traditional)

    a. ■

    b.□

34. Do you quickly

a. solve problems for those inside when you're coming from outside (change-driven) **or**

b. refuse to spend your treasures to develop new ideas that might fail? (traditional)

   a. ■

   b. □

35. Would you rather listen to and learn from philosophers that

a. predict a future in which old habits are replaced with new ones (change-driven) **or**

b. are only interested in experiencing one day at a time? (traditional)

   a. □

   b. ■

Road from the Altay to China and west to Asia Minor. This character is your alter ego and takes on your own personality as he solves problems or crimes.

It is also known that 30,000 Alans (an Iranic-speaking tribe) formed the royal guard (Asud) of the Yuan court in Dadu (Beijing) China.

✎ *The 10 Choices:*

THE CHOICES:	
Grounded	Verve
Rational	Enthusiastic
Decisive	Investigative
Loner	Outgoing
Traditional	Change-Driven

1. To write your story, would you prefer to

   a. go to the archives and find out who really was the first ruler of the tribe. You'd start with the book references listed in Wikipedia online, and then consult your own language translations, if any, of the book titled, *The Turks*, by *Güzel, Hasan Celal; Oğuz, C. Cem (2002), The Turks, 2, Ankara: Yeni Türkiye,* ISBN 9756782552. *Then you'd look for* translated letters sent by Sui to the Kağan asking to send her a young husband (down-to-earth) **or**

   b. dig deeper and find out the connections

between Chinese and the Turkic documents, to read about who was the first Kağan of the Göktürks. You'd look up other books listed online and in libraries on the history of Turks and Turanians. Then you'd look up wolf hand symbols and signs among other cultures from India to Native Americans and Siberians.

Then you'd read the emotions and gestures, the body language of the wolf hand symbols to see what they mean and where they originated—Siberia, or the Altay (also spelled Altai) or beyond to Mongolia. Then you'd deduce why Sui doesn't want to marry the Sogdian refugee that she has been promised to by her father who is destitute and caught in the famine of the mini-ice age of 6th century Altay. (**verve**)

a. □

b. □

2. **Would you be more interested in researching history and writing about**

a. the closeness of the relationship that surfaced between the Huns and the Turks from the sixth century back to 4,000 years ago (**enthusiastic**) **or**

b. analyze the business deals and diplomatic events between these equal powers to see who was winning the race to becoming the superpower of the century? (**rational**)

a. ☐

b. ☐

3. **Are you more interested in the fact that**

a. A Turanian Khatun (Queen) who wrote all her letters in an Altay (Altai) dialect, (**down-to-earth**) **or**

b. To find out whether the Kağan's father, was so admired or so hated after his death because he worshipped the lucky charm, a tamga, of a wolf spirit or whether he worshipped a tamga of a white horse or a hawk. (**verve**)

    a. ☐

    b. ☐

4. **Would you rather write about**

a. The sons of a royal Ashina clan being adopted, sent as a gift from Mongolia during their Altay step father's festival of his many years of reign (**enthusiastic**) **or**

b. You'd prefer to solve the mystery of why some of the sons of the royal Ashina are *thought* to be associated with the Tribe of Levi by some, according to whether they have a specific sequence of the 'Y' chromosome sequence that has the letter 'Q' in it that may link some royal Ashina to some Levites from Eastern Europe. Ashinas are said to come from the Suo nation, north of Xiongnu (**rational**)?

    a. □

    b. □

5. **You are a Khatun (Altay Queen). Would you rather**

    a. exercise your right as a widow to claim an unmarried Altay prince (**enthusiastic**) **or**

    b. marry your late husband's male nanny because it's only right and fair to restore an Altay Turanian to Turania's throne? (**rational**)

        a. □

        b. □

6. **An Altay princess of a vast stretch of land she calls Turania in the 6th century who is a widow may have written to her father-in-law to send her another of his sons for marriage to her. As a writer of her life story, would you rather**

    a. create a laundry list of princes that she must interview and screen in a dating game (**down-to-earth**) **or**

    b. create a story where she rides 1,000 miles on a donkey to run away from her servant after he forces her to marry him and has magical adventures disguised as a 14-year old boy studying philosophy and alchemy

speak or perform? (**decisive**)

a. □

b. □

15. If you were a Turanian Khatun (Queen), would you prefer to

a. receive warnings well in advance and without surprises that your late husband's nanny and regent is planning to get rid of you and marry another Queen of a different Tribe (adoptive grandmother of your late husband); so you could conveniently disappear (**decisive**) **or**

b. adapt to last-moment changes by never getting down to your last man or your last bowl of fermented mare's milk? (**investigative**)

a. □

b. □

16. As a scribe, artist, and poet in early medieval Turania would you

a. feel constrained by the Kağan's time schedules and deadlines (due dates) (**investigative**) **or**

b. set realistic timetables and juggle priorities? (decisive)

a. □

b. □

17. As the Kağan's widow, do you feel bound to

a. go with social custom, do the activities itemized on the social calendar, and marry your dead husband's unmarried brother because it's organized according to a plan (**decisive**) or

b. go with the flow of the relationship, deal with issues as they arise, marry a Khazar warrior from another tribe, marry a Royal Ashina from Xiongnu, or simply make no commitments or assumptions about what's the right thing to do because time changes plans and you just prefer to wait until more information is available? (**investigative**)

a. □

b. □

18. You're the Ashina Kağan reading the Altay Turanian widow's desperate letter in your own country of Xiongu. Is your reply to the Altay (Turanian) Khatun (Queen) more likely to be

a. one brief, concise, and to the point letter (rational) **or**

b. one sociable, friendly, empathetic and time-consuming letter? (enthusiastic)

a. □

b. □

19. **You're the Göktürk Kağan contemplating who most wants to replace you with an Ashina ruler. You make a list of**

a. the pros and cons of each person close to you (**rational**) **or**

b. varied comments from friends and relatives on what they say behind your back regarding how your influence them and what they want from you. (**enthusiastic**)

    a. ☐

    b. ☐

20. **The human body is like the Silk Road, you have been taught. You're the great healer who came all the way along the Silk Road from Cathay trying to heal with acupuncture needles as your tools, working your way along the energy points of chi to help the Göktürk Kağan in medieval Turania. Would you rather investigate**

a. the tried and true facts about energy points (**down-to-earth**) **or**

b. want to see what's in the overall picture as part of your expertise before you place the acupuncture needles at specific energy points that the Göktürk Kağan calls his clues? (**verve**)

    a. ☐

    b. ☐

21. **You're a Silk Road traveling healer looking for the energy meridians or points on the Göktürk Kağan's older brother. Your job is to restore his energy in his golden wise years. You**

a. seldom make errors of detail when looking for clues to heal such as taking notice of the Göktürk Kağan's rival wedding present to the young, healthy Khatun (Queen)--her freshly inscribed tamga charm for good luck, an amulet of a white horse. (**down-to-earth**) or

b. prefer more innovative work like writing secret love poems to the Queen disguised as prayers to the wolf goddess and watching for the sacred horse's spirit to escape through the ice cave hole dug into the frozen tundra near one of the Altay mountains. (**verve**)

    a. ☐
    b. ☐

22. **As a scribe and healer, you become**

a. tired when you work alone all day in a dimly-lighted *yurt* (**outgoing**) or

b. tired when the latest Göktürk Kağan interrupts your concentration on your work to demand that you greet and entertain his guests all evening at banquets with wolf hand shapes as shadow symbols on the walls of the yurt near a lamp of fire. (**loner**).

    a. □

    b. □

23. **When the Khatun (Queen) asks you as a healer to write love poems for her that she can hand to the Göktürk Kağan, you**

a. create the ideas for your poems by long discussions with the Queen (**outgoing**) **or**

b. prefer to be alone when you reach deep down inside your spirit to listen to what your wolf goddess (soul entities) tell you as the only resource for writing metaphors. (**loner**)

    a. □

    b. □

24. **You are in medieval Turania investigating the death of an elderly Göktürk Kağan and prefer to**

a. question many different foreigners and locals at boisterous celebrations in different languages (**outgoing**) **or**

b. disregard outside events and look inside the family history/genealogy rune inscriptions on a stone for the culprit. (**loner**)

a. □

b. □

25. The next Göktürk Kağan, at a young age asks you to develop ideas for him about how to act when ascending the throne so young. You prefer to develop ideas through

a. reflection, meditation, and shamanic prayer to tanri/tengri (**loner**) **or**

b. discussions and interviews among the Göktürk Kağan's playmates on what makes the Göktürk Kağan laugh. (**outgoing**)

a. □

b. □

26. As an Altay healer and Shaman, you are

a. rarely cautious about the family position of those with whom you socialize as long as they are kind, righteous people who do good deeds (**outgoing**) **or**

b. seeking one person with power to raise you from healer to the next Göktürk Kağan of Turania, if only the present Göktürk Kağan would ask your advice. (**loner**)

a. □

b. □

27. **You are a sculptor, healer, and scribe in early medieval Turania when the Gök-türk Kağan asks you to carve a name for yourself using Ataly runes on a special stone with magical properties that bears the image of a wolf and is a special representation of its owner. Would you**

a. inscribe the Turanic rune that means 'remote' (**loner**) **or**

b. choose a special name for yourself that means, "He who shares time easily with many foreigners along the Silk Road, beyond Altay?" (**outgoing**)

    a. □

    b. □

28. **As an ancient healer (Shaman) in Central Asia, do you work better when you**

a. spend your day off where no one can see you asking the sacred wolf goddess why her teeth are so sharp if she is supposed to be more intelligent at finding food than the horizontal-toothed sacred horse on that tamga amulet to tengri/tanri (**loner**) **or**

b. spend your free time training teams of apprentice Shaman-healers using the acupuncture needles you learned how to use before you left your familiar trade route to visit Cathay to keep traveling along the Silk Road to the *Kara Kum* desert? (**outgoing**)

   a. ☐

   b. ☐

29. If you discovered a new land, would you build your cities upon

a. your wise elders' principles as they always have worked well before (**traditional**) **or**

b. unfamiliar cargo that traders brought from afar to civilize your land? (**change-driven**)

   a.☐

   b.☐

30. Do you depict the Göktürk Kağan's victories on a stone in Turanian runes exactly as

a. surviving witnesses from both sides recounted the events (**change-driven**) **or**

b. the Göktürk Kağan wants people to see? (**traditional**)

   a.☐

   b.☐

31. If you're self-motivated, would you avoid learning from your Tarkhan (military leader) because

a. your overseer doesn't keep up with the times (**change-driven**) or

b. your overseer doesn't let you follow in your father's footsteps? (**traditional**)

a.□

b.□

32. Would you prefer to

a. train healers, Shamans and scribes because your father taught you how to do it well (**traditional**) or

b. move quickly from one project to another forever? (**change-driven**)

a.□

b.□

33. Do you feel like an outsider when

a. you think *more* about going back along the Silk road to China or staying in the Altay in the future than about *current* healing chores in Turania (**change-driven**) or

b. do you think more about the stress of being of service to invaders from many different lands along the Silk Road that have now replaced your forefathers' familiar Chinese foods with unfamiliar dairy cuisine from Altay and Xiongnu such as fermented mare's milk? (**traditional**)

a.☐

b.☐

34. Do you quickly

a. solve problems for those inside when you're coming from outside (**change-driven**) **or**

b. refuse to spend your treasures to develop new ideas that might fail? (**traditional**)

a.☐

b.☐

35. Would you rather listen to and learn from Turanian, Ashina, and Chinese philosophers that

a. predict a future in which old habits are replaced with new ones (**change-driven**) **or**

b. are only interested in experiencing one day at a time? (**traditional**)

a.☐

b.☐

Self-Scoring the Test

Add up the number of answers for each of the following ten writing style traits for the 35 questions. There are seven questions for each group. The ten categories (your ten choices) are made up of five opposite pairs.

Down-to-earth	**Verve**
Rational	**Enthusiastic**
Decisive	**Investigative**
Loner	**Outgoing**
Traditional	**Change-Driven**

Then put the numbers for each answer next to the categories.

1. Total Down-to-earth	6. Total Verve
2. Total Rational	7. Total Enthusiastic
3. Total Decisive	8. Total Investigative
4. Total Loner	9. Total Outgoing
5. Total Traditional	10. Total Change-Driven

To get your score, you're only adding up the number of answers for each of the 10 categories (five pairs) above. Note that there are seven questions for each of the five pairs (or 10 designations). There are 35 questions. Seven questions times five categories equal 35 questions. Keep the number of questions you design for each category equal. The other assessments containing 35 questions (in this book) are similar and are scored with the same self-scoring process as this assessment.

℘

Look at the other previous sample 35-question assessments in this book that have their boxes checked. Note that in them, the four highest numbers of answers are enthusiastic, investigative, imaginative loner. This last but not least test would score the same way.

Choose the highest numbers first as having the most importance (or weight) in your writing style preference. Your score would be your own *creative writing **style** and the way you plot your character's actions, interests, and goals,* one example of many (for fiction writing and specifically mystery writing) could be an ***enthusiastic investigative vivacious (verve-with-imagination) loner***. **Your five personality letters would be: E I V L C.** (Scramble the letters to make a word to remember, the name Clive, in this case.) There are no 'right' or 'wrong' answers. Your writing style is individual and can be made up of your personal letters or preferences. You write according to your personality choices, writing style, and the behavior and environment of your characters.

Note that in the *first sample scored test* in this book (*using the first assessment's setting in ancient Egypt*) there is a tie between C and V. Both have a score of '5'. However, since 'V' (verve) which signifies vivacious imagination with gusto competes with 'C', being change-driven, the 'verve' in the vivacious personality wracked with creative imagination would wither in a traditional corporation that emphasizes routinely running a tight ship. Traditional firms seek to imitate successful corporations of the past that worked well and still work. They don't need to be fixed often unless they make noise.

Instead, the dominantly change-driven creative individual would flourish better with a forward-looking,

Here's a sample scored assessment.

↔ *"Turanian Catalyst" Creative Writing Assessment*

You are an historical fiction adventure and intrigue **writer** working on a novel, play, or script that will eventually become a computer video game for young males and/or an interactive audio book of stories with clues for the Web about a Turanian *catalyst*, a person who *brings people together* to join territories, tribes, or interests based on common ancient ancestry or language group. The setting is in a city you will choose, located in medieval Asia Minor, Central Asia, along the Steppes, or in Mongolia. Your hero's name is Tumen Il-Kağan. The year is 551 of the Common Era. *According to ancient Chinese sources*, your hero's name means "cloud of smoke."

The plot of your story begins as Tumen gathers together a group of Turkic people who live in the Altay Mountains. Their village is very difficult to reach and is called Ergenikon. The scene opens in the cloud-whipped valleys beneath the Altay Mountains.

This person, avatar, or hero has unending adventures trying to create a vast territory of united Steppe Peoples speaking related languages. The hero calls this vast legacy of land, *Turania.*

Your first Göktürk Kağan travels between various places in Central Asia and Mongolia and is exposed to Buddhism from Chinese travelers he meets along the Silk Road. The hero is a **Göktürk Kağan.** You can make your main character or protagonist native to the Steppes or anywhere in Central Asia, Asia Minor, or Mongolia, but being of a Turkic-speaking language group. His mascot is the grey wolf, and the grey wolf has a white she-wolf companion. So the hero is seen walking with two wolves on each side of him signaling people he meets with the wolf hand sign.

Your protagonist/hero, Tumen Il-Kaḡan, is in a race against time because the area is in the grips of a mini-ice age. The hero travels to teach *wolf hand symbols* to fellow Turanians across Central Asia from the area on the West near the Black Sea (Pontus) all the way beyond the Caspian Sea's East Coast to the Altay Mountains, along the Silk Road, and on to Mongolia and western China. The protagonist (main character) travels the Silk Road from his or her native land in the Altay Mountains.

He sets out on a road that leads to Western China and spreads the *wolf hand sign* greetings that was said to originate in Siberia thousands of years ago.

Across the Silk Road that the Byzantine Romans used, a teenaged Altay widow named Sui asked help from Tumen to prevent her from being forced into an unwilling marriage with a Sogdian refugee because the Sogdian refugees fled to Tumen's territory. Shah Anushirvan Khorasau I. (closer in territory and language groups to Persia) persecuted the Zurvanites. Sui wants to marry the protagonist of your story. But the Sogdian refugee wants to marry Sui for power, so he can overtake the Kaḡan.

You have a bit of a Samson and Delilah theme somewhat. You can reverse the plot and make it a Delilah and Samson theme. The question is, according to your personality preferences, how will you write this interactive story, according to your writing style preferences?

Tumen meets Ashina, one of ten sons born to a grey she-wolf in north Gaochang. Ashina also was a ruling dynasty and tribe of ancient Turks in the 6th century. The Ashina's leader, Bumin Khan had descendants that revolted against the Rouran. His brother, Istemi, ruled over the east and west of the Göktürk empire.

Ashina's ancestors came from the Suo nation, north of Xiongnu. Chinese legends say Ashina's mother was a wolf and the goddess of a particular season. The Ashina tribe of skilled military archers were descended from one archer named Shemo.

This Shemo fell in love with a sea goddess near Ashide cave, according to the Book of Zhou (Lighu Defen, et al. Also see the Book of Sui (Wei Zheng, et al.) The Ashina royal family was composed of many different ethnic groups. They arose out of the Pingliang soldiers from eastern Gansu.

So you have a story line right there of why they would want to use the wolf hand symbols or signs made (in profile view) with the middle finger and ring finger pressed to the thumb to signify the nose and mouth of the wolf with the pinky and index finger straight up to signify the wolf's ears. With all this information, how will you organize your story?

✎ Clues

The leading character is the Kağan who also is a scribe in several languages he's learned from his travels in Altay and along the entire length of the Silk Road between Western China, the Altay, and Byzantine Constantinople. This is the 6th century. In the Altay, nature is worshipped. As he travels closer to China, he is influenced by Buddhism.

This first Kağan of the Göktürks has inherited wealth from an ancestral line of Altay royalty. He's a male healer and scribe, age 20, living in the royal yurt. He grew up learning many languages as he traveled the Silk Road from the Altay to China and west to Asia Minor. This character is your alter ego and takes on your own personality as he solves problems or crimes.

It is also known that 30,000 Alans (an Iranic-speaking tribe) formed the royal guard (Asud) of the Yuan court in Dadu (Beijing) China.

↜ *The 10 Choices:*

THE CHOICES:	
Grounded	Verve
Rational	Enthusiastic
Decisive	Investigative
Loner	Outgoing
Traditional	Change-Driven

1. To write your story, would you prefer to

a. go to the archives and find out who really was the first ruler of the tribe. You'd start with the book references listed in Wikipedia online, and then consult your own language translations, if any, of the book titled, *The Turks*, by *Güzel, Hasan Celal; Oğuz, C. Cem (2002), The Turks, 2, Ankara: Yeni Türkiye,* ISBN 9756782552. *Then you'd look for* translated letters sent by Sui to the Kağan asking to send her a young husband (down-to-earth) **or**

b. dig deeper and find out the connections between Chinese and the Turkic documents, to read about who was the first Kağan of the Göktürks. You'd look up other books listed online and in libraries on the history of Turks and Turanians. Then you'd look up wolf hand symbols and signs among other cultures from India to Native Americans and Siberians.

Then you'd read the emotions and gestures, the body language of the wolf hand symbols to see what they mean and where they originated—Siberia, or the Altay (also spelled Altai) or beyond to Mongolia. Then you'd deduce why Sui doesn't want to marry the Sogdian refugee that she has been promised to by her father who is destitute and caught in the famine of the mini-ice age of 6th century Altay. (verve)

a. □

b. ■

2. **Would you be more interested in researching history and writing about**

a. the closeness of the relationship that surfaced between the Huns and the Turks from the sixth century back to 4,000 years ago (enthusiastic) or

b. analyze the business deals and diplomatic

events between these equal powers to see who was winning the race to becoming the superpower of the century? (rational)

a. ■

b. □

3. **Are you more interested in the fact that**

a. A Turanian Khatun (Queen) who wrote all her letters in an Altay (Altai) dialect, (down-to-earth) **or**

b. To find out whether the Kağan's father, was so admired or so hated after his death because he worshipped the lucky charm, a tamga, of a wolf spirit or whether he worshipped a tamga of a white horse or a hawk. (verve)

a. ■

b. □

4. **Would you rather write about**

a. The sons of a royal Ashina clan being adopted, sent as a gift from Mongolia during their Altay step father's festival of his many years of reign (**enthusiastic**) **or**

b. You'd prefer to solve the mystery of why some of the sons of the royal Ashina are *thought* to be associated with the Tribe of Levi by some, according to whether they have a specific sequence of the 'Y' chromosome sequence that has the letter 'Q' in it that may link some royal Ashina to some Levites from Eastern Europe. Ashinas are said to come from the Suo nation, north of Xiongnu (**rational**)?

a. □

b. ■

5. **You are a Khatun (Altay Queen). Would you rather**

a. exercise your right as a widow to claim an unmarried Altay prince (enthusiastic) **or**

b. marry your late husband's male nanny because it's only right and fair to restore an Altay Turanian to Turania's throne? (rational)

a. ■

b. □

6. **An Altay princess of a vast stretch of land she calls Turania in the 6ᵗʰ century who is a widow may have written to her father-in-law to send her another of his sons for marriage to her. As a writer of her life story, would you rather**

a. create a laundry list of princes that she must interview and screen in a dating game (down-to-earth) **or**

b. create a story where she rides 1,000 miles on a donkey to run away from her servant after he forces her to marry him and has magical adventures disguised as a 14-year old boy studying philosophy and alchemy with Chinese acupuncture healers and astrologers she meets in her travels at the far end of the Silk Road? (verve)

a. □

b. ■

7. **Are you more interested in ending your story with**

a. A Turanian prince marrying an Altay young widow, then taking the Kağan's adoptive grandmother, (you might create a story about a mythical Queen Yildiz) as a second wife, so that you have closure and an ending for your story (decisive) **or**

b. would you rather let your story remain open for serialization, since the Kağan's widow is never heard from again after she marries her late husband's regent and nanny. He then marries a different princess, from the royal Ashina tribe, since the fate of the Turanian Kağan's widow after marrying the regent is not recorded in history? (investigative)

a. □

b. ■

8. **If you were a Turanian, would you prefer to**

   a. decide immediately to obey the Ashina Kağan and leave your own country to marry the widowed Queen of the Turanians because duty required it, knowing you'll probably be killed when you arrive by the same person who killed the former Kağan, (decisive) **or**

   b. stall for time as long as possible, waiting for validated information to arrive regarding the diplomatic climate between the Ashina and the Turanians (since Turanians are Altay and the Ashina are similar, but from Xiongnu)? (investigative).

      a. □

      b. ■

9. **You are the Göktürk Kağan adopted in infancy as a gift from an Ashina ruler because the Khatun (queen) had six daughters. If you were Kağan, would you**

   a. speak in the Altay language in front of your Xiongu-area dialect speaking Ashina Regent, thereby possibly inflaming the nationalism in him (investigative) **or**

   b. plan and organize methodically to have a whole line of people close to you from your own country of origin, Altay and Turania originating in Central Asia) rather than from the lair of the wolf-goddess mother that legend has told you was the place of your origin? (decisive)

a. ☐

b. ■

10. Would you rather write about

a. terms of the treaty between the peoples of Turania and Ashina of Xiongu based on the facts provided by records (down-to-earth) **or**

b. the theories set in motion when the Ashina Kağan marries the Altay Kağan's widow and soon after, the widow disappears, and the Ashina marries another Khatun (Queen) mythically named Yildiz, the so-called daughter of a mother goddess of the wolf tribes that use wolf hand symbols to show loyalty to one another's similar language tribes? (verve)

a. ☐

b. ■

11. Do you like writing about

a. enigmas or puzzles set in motion by symbols on intimate funerary equipment in a mystery novel (rational) **or**

b. why so many other Turanians use wolf hand symbols or signs where the index finger and the pinky are raised to represent the wolf's ears while the thumb crosses over the folded middle and ring fingers—or both the Turanians and the Ashinas of Xiongnu and Central Asia use the wolf finger symbol of a wolf face in profile where the middle and ring fingers and thumb form the long wolf's snout while the upheld pinky and index fingers form the wolf's ears? (enthusiastic)

a. □

b. ■

12. **A *tag line* shows the mood/emotion in the voice--how a character speaks or acts. Are you more interested in**

a. compiling, counting, and indexing *citations* or *quotes* from how-to books for writers (down-to-earth) **or**

b. compiling *tag lines* that explain in fiction dialogue the specific behaviors or gestures such as, "Yes, he replied timorously."? (verve)

a. □

b. ■

13. **Would you rather write**

a. dialog (enthusiastic) **or**

b. description? (rational)

a. ■

b. □

14. To publicize your writing, would you rather

a. give spectacular presentations or shows without preparation or prior notice (investigative) **or**

b. have to prepare a long time in advance to speak or perform? (decisive)

a. ■
b. □

15. If you were a Turanian Khatun (Queen), would you prefer to

a. receive warnings well in advance and without surprises that your late husband's nanny and regent is planning to get rid of you and marry another Queen of a different Tribe (adoptive grandmother of your late husband); so you could conveniently disappear (decisive) **or**

b. adapt to last-moment changes by never getting down to your last man or your last bowl of fermented mare's milk? (investigative)

a. ■
b. □

16. As a scribe, artist, and poet in early medieval Turania would you

a. feel constrained by the Kağan's time schedules and deadlines (due dates) (investigative) **or**

tions on a stone for the culprit. (loner)

a. ☐

b. ■

25. **The next Göktürk Kağan, at a young age asks you to develop ideas for him about how to act when ascending the throne so young. You prefer to develop ideas through**

a. reflection, meditation, and prayer (loner) **or**

b. discussions and interviews among the Göktürk Kağan's playmates on what makes the Göktürk Kağan laugh. (outgoing)

a. ■

b. ☐

26. **As an Altay healer and Shaman, you are**

a. rarely cautious about the family position of those with whom you socialize as long as they are kind, righteous people who do good deeds (outgoing) **or**

b. seeking one person with power to raise you from healer to the next Göktürk Kağan of Turania, if only the present Göktürk Kağan would ask your advice. (loner)

a. ☐

b. ■

27. **You are a sculptor, healer, and scribe in early medieval Turania when the Göktürk**

Kağan asks you to carve a name for yourself using Ataly runes on a special stone with magical properties that bears the image of a wolf and is a special representation of its owner. Would you

a. inscribe the Turanic rune that means 're-mote' (loner) **or**

b. choose a special name for yourself that means, "He who shares time easily with many foreigners along the Silk Road, beyond Altay?" (outgoing)

    a. ☐

    b. ■

28. As an ancient healer (Shaman) in Central Asia, do you work better when you

a. spend your day off where no one can see you asking the sacred wolf goddess why her teeth are so sharp if she is supposed to be more intelligent at finding food than the horizontal-toothed sacred horse on that tamga amulet to tengri/tanri (**loner**) **or**

b. spend your free time training teams of apprentice Shaman-healers using the acupuncture needles you learned how to use before you left your familiar trade route to visit Cathay to keep traveling along the Silk Road to the *Kara Kum* desert? (**outgoing**)

a. ■

b. ☐

29. If you discovered a new land, would you build your cities upon

a. your wise elders' principles as they always have worked well before (traditional) **or**

b. unfamiliar cargo that traders brought from afar to civilize your land? (change-driven)

    a. ☐

    b. ■

30. Do you depict the Göktürk Kağan's victories on a stone in Turanian runes exactly as

a. surviving witnesses from both sides recounted the events (change-driven) **or**

b. the Göktürk Kağan wants people to see? (traditional)

    a. ☐

    b. ■

31. If you're self-motivated, would you avoid learning from your Tarkhan (military leader) because

a. your overseer doesn't keep up with the times (change-driven) **or**

b. your overseer doesn't let you follow in your father's footsteps? (traditional)

    a. ■

b. □

32. Would you prefer to

a. train healers, Shamans and scribes because your father taught you how to do it well (traditional) **or**

b. move quickly from one project to another forever? (change-driven)

    a. □

    b. ■

33. Do you feel like an outsider when

a. you think *more* about going back along the Silk road to China or staying in the Altay in the future than about *current* healing chores in Turania (change-driven) **or**

b. do you think more about the stress of being of service to invaders from many different lands along the Silk Road that have now replaced your forefathers' familiar Chinese foods with unfamiliar dairy cuisine from Altay and Xiongu such as fermented mare's milk? (traditional)

    a. ■

    b. □

34. Do you quickly

a. solve problems for those inside when you're coming from outside (change-driven) **or**

b. refuse to spend your treasures to develop

new ideas that might fail? (traditional)

a. ■

b. □

35. **Would you rather listen to and learn from Turanian, Ashina, and Chinese philosophers that**

a. predict a future in which old habits are replaced with new ones (change-driven) **or**

b. are only interested in experiencing one day at a time? (traditional)

a. ■

b. □

When you add up the sample scored assessment, the writer prefers a change-driven *enthusiastic investigative vivacious (verve-with-imagination) loner* approach **to solving problems for his or her main characters. Your five personality letters for your varied writing style aptitude and/or your character's personality preferences would be: E I V L C.** (Scramble the letters to make a word to remember, the name Clive, in this case.)

↭ *Scores*

Total Down-to-earth	0	Total Verve	0
Total Rational	0	Total Enthusiastic	7
Total Decisive	0	Total Investigative	7
Total Loner	4	Total Outgoing	3

Total Traditional   2   Total Change-Driven 5

Note that there is a tie between C (change-driven) and V (verve). Both have a score of '5'. However, since 'V' (verve) which signifies vivacious imagination with gusto competes with 'C', being change-driven, the 'verve' in the vivacious personality wracked with creative imagination would wither in a traditional corporation that emphasizes routinely running a tight ship. Traditional firms seek to imitate successful corporations of the past that worked well and still work. They don't need to be fixed often unless they make noise.

Instead, the dominantly change-driven creative individual would flourish better with a forward-looking, trend-setting creative corporation and build security from flexibility of job skill. When in doubt, turn to action verbs to communicate your 'drive.' If you're misplaced, you won't connect as well with co-workers and may be dubbed "a loose cannon."

You know you're writing in the right genre when your personality connects with the genre of fiction or creative nonfiction readers and groups to share meaning. Communication is the best indicator of your personality matching a character's traits. It's all about connecting more easily with readers who enjoy the characters you create based on your preferences and the character's actions.

PART V

Take the "Sailing the Ancient Mediterranean with Paul of Patmos, Calliope, and a Friendly Dog, Xanthe" Creative Writing Assessment

First Read the Back Story and Clues Below to Get a Handle:

The Antikythera Device:

✦ Clues

I am the time traveler, Calliope of Patmos, whose family invented, owned, and gave up to the sea, one of the rare, Greek *antikythera* celestial navigation gears used for nearly three thousand years by Greek and later, Roman sailors. The *antikythera* device served as a mechanism of complicated gears physically representing the Callippic and Saros astronomical cycles.

It's not only gears I wanted to mesh. Intimate glimpses of the human condition may be found in numerous art galleries.

In the first century, I lived on the small Greek island of Patmos, surrounded by the Aegean Sea at the time our neighbor, the white-haired Paul of Tarsus, once sought a bowl of vegetable broth at my family tavern of sustenance serving stews for the sensibilities.

My beliefs here on Patmos that year emphasized good deeds rather than complex creeds. I had been a builder of dreams seeking practical applications, but so far ahead of my century, that I actually found time-travel a gift of destiny.

For me back then, the daughter of a proper Greek widow who could write well. My mother copied numerous scrolls and letters that Paul of Tarsus on Patmos brought into the tavern. As a follower, mother would give me copies of some letters. My widowed mother committed herself to faith, keeping the family together in spite of all odds, and putting bread on the table and always an extra bowl for Paul's dog, Xanthe.

Here on Patmos, the family goal focused solely on commitment. We all followed Paul when he came near our tavern for his bowl of broth. We listened to the whisperings of his talks and read his writings. And yet I longed to be an explorer and observer of comparative thought in faraway places and future times.

As girl of sixteen alone in the world, and having arrived as the new tutor in a wealthy Roman household villa in the far west Neapolis, the only way I could study the human condition consisted of gawking at works of art where I could reflect. Our art... I kept a treasure hidden with me, the prized *antikythera* navigation gears and astronomical calendar.

For it is written: Five hundred years before that time of Paul, my father's father-fourteen generations removed, invented the *antikythera* celestial navigation device, and in those years, it served well as my treasure.

Not only had I been granted Roman citizenship because of the treasured Greek family name appearing in writing in three languages as the celestial navigation gear's inventor, but now, on my first job as Greek language, poetry writing, and history tutor to a child in the wealthiest Roman family in Neapolis, where many people also spoke Greek.

The older child had a separate mathematics tutor, and a tutor for engineering and building bridges. But I was assigned to teach the five-year old to read, speak, and write poetry as a healing tool. I spoke the many languages of trade.

So begins my proper passage at sixteen from adolescence to womanhood as a tutor in ancient Rome, the last outpost of civilization to my senses. See any similarity in this holistic adventure to a timeless search for the perfect nurturing mother?

Look at your deeds, I heard my mother once say to Paul of Tarsus when he lived and wrote on Patmos, the island of my birth. I told Paul that our art shows us the human condition. And peace in the home feeds the growth of consciousness.

Now, I found myself in Rome, hidden in villa gardens so far from my family. Yet my letters to Paul where still sent as often as my letters to my own mother whose life focused on commitment to family and faith.

Often, I wore that plain iron ring and carried the scrolls that set me apart from the denizens of slaves who also served as tutors. Because of my citizen-ring and the signed papers, none of my father had ever been slaves of the Romans.

Look at me at sixteen, a Roman citizen with signed deeds to my ancestor's *antikythera* invention attributed to my family and me as the only heir. Yet as a proper Greek girl, and not a slave, invitations abounded to dine as the daughter of the long missing-at-sea Apollodorus.

There were no more men left in my family to work as well-paid Greek architects contracted to draft the plans for villas in Neapolis for the wealthiest aristocrats as there had been for generations. I passed the precious time writing letters to Paul of Tarsus on Patmos as he wrote letters of his own that one day I would read.

And I, never really alone at sixteen with my mother's copies of Paul's letters nearby, spent a few nights on special feast days at the house of Salonius, a wealthy Roman and distant relative of the prosperous Cornelius family. His vast fortunes came from building many summer villas for still wealthier Romans in Neapolis overlooking the sea. Salonius, with wife and children shared this large villa.

At those times of my first few days on trial for employment as a tutor to my five-year-old playmate, Octavia, I lied awake, well protected, I thought, close to Octavia and to her rotund mother, Velia, an Etruscan who married into the old Latium family of Salonius Cornelius. As chaperoned children, we slept in the roped, rutted wool and feathered torus next to Velia.

"What's that you're holding?" Velia asked me.

"My Antikythera device," I said timorously. "It's a navigational tool for Greek sailors."

"Give me that!" Velia quickly removed it from my tiny fingers and pocketed the device.

"But it belongs to my father. It's been in our family for four hundred years." I quickly grabbed it back from her hands and placed it inside my goatskin purse.

"Well, now it's mine. Give it here." Pursy Velia huffed, pulling the gears from the sack strung around my waist.

"Go ahead keep it then," I sighed. "If you don't know how to use it right, there's the danger that any ship that misuses it might sink. I must not lose this. It's all that stands between my freedom and slavery. My Roman citizenship scrolls would be worthless without proof that my family line invented the device."

"Then I'll sell it so you won't envy this evil eye in front of me," Velia teased.

I used my own family members as models by memorizing the fruits of our family slogan of deeds, not creeds. I jostled the words to Velia without understanding their impact.

"Our Greek family travels only to study and understand the human condition for inner peace. And you can only learn about the human condition by studying what is in the art galleries of all peoples. Our goal is peace in the home.

You have to practice it in every room if you ever want to grow world peace. That's why you must return the *antikythera* to me or my mother or our friend, Paul of Tarsus who is now living on Patmos. The gears point the celestial direction of navigation. It belongs on a ship. Our family invented it for the purpose of growing peace."

"You grow peace, like a vine or a tree?" Velia looked up in surprise, grinning crookedly, but not smiling with her eyes.

"That's right," I told her eagerly. "You heal yourself into peace in an art gallery, not in a pantheon. Otherwise you're talking to yourself. Don't you know that the purpose of life is to understand the human condition?"

"You certainly can't do anything about it." Velia squealed with impatience. "You're just a crupper, a strap holding a riding saddle steady," Velia said impatiently. "I've heard about Paul of Tarsus. And I know all about your poor, widowed mother. You know what you are? You're trying to steady yourself on what Paul has taught you. I heard him speak on Patmos."

"So you know his followers."

"I'm afraid of what he says," Velia sighed. "As an Etruscan married into this Roman world, I've heard

Velia had saved a few sesterces from the pittance she told me that Salonius gave her each morning and bought Octavia two stringed musical instruments for her fifth birthday.

I hadn't been home to look at the presents my loving father bought me, but that surprise could wait. I spent the night after Octavia's birthday party simply because Cornelius was close friends with his most important scribe, Salonius, and my father had work to discuss with Cornelius. We all spent the night in the house of Salonius.

And now rage overtook Salonius as if possessed by an angry bull. "We Romans don't worship animals, nor do we let them pollute our households. Once in a while our Egyptian slaves let their kittens ransack the kitchens to scare off rats and buzzing insects."

Yet the look on Salonius's face was that of a mad, starved animal charging his prey. Normally he was a charming man to Cornelius, or in public, but at home, I've seen him change in an instant before the eyes of his wife and children. And an hour later, he denied anything was amiss.

When Salonius finished smashing the smaller turtle lyres, he went for Octavia's wooden kithera with its special echoing sound box, and then for her larger, barbitos lyres. These were presents my father brought Octavia for her birthday. Then Salonius shouted in pain as he kicked his bare foot through the thick and solid arms of the eleven-stringed phorminx lyre and the array of extra sheep-gut strings that Velia purchased for her older son's seventh birthday.

After a year or two of lessons, he gave it up. For years it had stood among her son's undusted toys, forgotten, until Velia asked me if I wanted it and told me the story of how Hermes invented the lyre and how many years it remained in her family.

I did want it at first, until I realized that Octavia wanted it more. So I made sure it stayed with Velia's family. I told my father not to bring it to our house, even if Velia offered it to us once more.

Salonius put his foot through the paintings and other instruments brought for Octavia's birthday. Finally, he grabbed the Egyptian kitchen slave's striped kitten that lost its way and wandered into Velia's room and held its belly against the hot pipes being installed in the new indoor bathhouse, until it stopped meowing.

I looked in on Octavia's mother, but Velia didn't move or respond to my presence. She laid there, one arm over the sobbing Octavia crouching against her mother. Velia gazed unblinking at the ceiling, and Octavia had told me many times that her mother said she had given up all effort.

I would never give up trying to find a life, an identity, a self, or a sense of belonging. I ran into the peristyle and Octavia jumped up and followed me, clinging to me for protection, a protection Velia didn't try to give to Octavia or to me as a guest in Salonius's home.

"Not my birthday presents. Don't smash my presents." Octavia cried, but now Salonius had spent his rage and returned, exhausted to his own room, but the respite didn't last for long.

The louder the sounds of her voice grew, the more angry Salonius became.

He began to chase Octavia first and then both of us all over his house waving this fasces a set of rods bound in the form of a bundle which contained an axe. Salonius's cousin, the bodyguard of a magistrate, carried the fasces.

He must have left it with Salonius for safekeeping when he went to visit his son's new baby in the countryside. Now he separated the axe from the rods and swung the axe over his head like a madman.

"If I catch you, I'll cripple you." Heads will roll before you'll become a tramp." He went for the axe in his private closet, putting the hammer away. Octavia and I scampered under a table and crouched there, sobbing. I didn't know how to defend myself or protect Octavia, being a scrawny boy scared beyond uttering a sound. Salonius seemed like a raging giant, a belching volcano spewing his poisonous gases at me and waving an axe.

"I'm sorry. I'm sorry, daddy," Octavia cried.

"Better you should be crippled than to be born a girl and make trouble for me.

I should have flushed her out into the Tiber. Better she wasn't made or born," Salonius ranted.

I sneaked back into Velia's sleeping quarters dragging Octavia by the hand. And we saw that Octavia's mother began to stir and shout to Salonius who still hunted us down from the next room.

"If I have to get up you two fighting make me sicker." She began to cough again. "Leave my baby alone." I shoved Octavia under the lectus and sidled under it myself. As children, even I at sixteen and she at five could crouch there, but a giant like Salonius would never be able to squeeze in that space.

Salonius, now angrier with Velia, took a swing at Octavia and me with the hammer, and missed because we moved deeper into the dark under the lectus. Salonius ran out of the room to retrieve his axe and in the instant of time I had to flee, Octavia and I darted from the kitchen and dashed out of the atrium into the garden.

There was a deep hole dug for an outdoor as well as an indoor privy and also a partially built storage room under construction. The workers had left for the night, and the hole in the garden soil was deep enough with enough dirt to cover us.

In the darkness, Salonius chased his daughter and me, gaining on me as I disappeared into the hole in the garden. We squeezed our small bodies into a partially filled dung pit, hiding inside back of an old barrel left there as it was still too new and unfinished to be used by anyone.

We covered ourselves with garden soil. I had a small space for air there in the barrel, and there was enough sawed out of it for me to see the lamp Salonius held high as he looked around for a few seconds, wild-eyed, wiping the beaded sweat on his upper lip on his forearm.

"If I catch you, I'll kill you," he shouted in a tremulous tone. I brought my puppy, Xanthe with me and held her snugly. She protected me, and I protected her and brought nourishment to the 12-week old *canis-lupus*. This animal friend given to me by Paul of Patmos must be protected from other beasts.

From between the wide slats of the broken barrel, I watched as he swung his axe overhead. As he passed a work table, Salonius slapped the ax against his thigh a couple of times. Then he sighed and left it on the table.

when their backs turned for a moment, the longer of the remnant ended up inside Velia's *stola*.

She waddled into the street to see the shoemaker. Velia and daughter sat down on a cushion before the shoemaker's shop.

"Give me that skinny foot," said the shopkeeper, trying to shove one of the new little sandals on Octavia's dirt-caked foot.

"The soles are too thin," Velia complained.

"Leave me alone!" Octavia whined, storming out of the shoe section. Octavia shouted a horrible obscenity at the shop keeper, the same word I heard her father call her last night as I looked over my shoulder at the shopkeeper's expression.

"That filthy rat," he stammered.

Breathless Velia caught up to her daughter in front of the public cistern where a line of slaves and poor citizens, all women, waited their turn to bring water into the small rooms they occupied around the market district called the *Subura*.

"Please, Velia, as an Etruscan, come back with me to Patmos where as a foreigner you'll be freer than you are here."

"I can't give up the villa."

The Subura, a place to shop here in Neapolis, is just like the same-named Subura in Rome. Both became a stench of dried blood, moldy fruit, rotting meat, sweat, urine, and manure.

In Rome when I was ten, our family took me to see it. To find the Subura in Rome, you enter the valley between the southern end of the Viminal and the western end of the Esquiline, or Oppius. Rome's Subura is connected with the forum by the Argiletum. It continues eastward between the Oppius and the Cispius by the Clivus Suburanus, ending at the Porta Esquilina. This Subura had the same look.

Now our litter ended up in the bakery district where we paused to find some shade. Velia chastised Octavia with a pointed finger. "Horse face, why by Jupiter did you say that?"

"He didn't have to call me skinny like in ugly," Octavia insisted, standing up for her reason for shouting an obscenity at the shoemaker. Velia threw her hands in the air out of frustration, or maybe she wanted to give up at that moment.

"Why did you have to wear that torn article of clothing outside the house? You're beginning to stink just like your father who's never taken a bath in years even with three pools.

The old stinker washes the bottom of his feet, his face and hands so Cornelius will think he's clean. He's afraid of water, says it makes his legs itch."

I listened in silence, then blurted. "Why doesn't he rub some oil on his skin if water makes it itch?"

Velia shook her head. While I observed but did not participate, she spent the day teaching Octavia how to steal clothing none of us needed from poor, old merchants who were overwhelmed with business or had no customers at all.

These merchants were too poor to own a slave to help them in their little shops, and most had sons who were killed in the wars. I felt sorry for them, but Velia only wanted this sensation she must have received from

Suddenly my son gave his sister a shove and then pulled her back to safety before she could let out a wail. But the five-year old heard the whisper."

"That's right," Octavia squealed. "He has no right to scare me like that."

Velia scratched her head.

"He denied it just like his father denies doing cruel acts. He started to sing to her. Then he lifted and dangled her as if to throw Octavia in the Tiber. She told me that she lashed out, flailing, screaming in terror. A passerby saw them horsing around, and she said he put her down harshly."

"I asked him why he did that," Octavia said, tossing her curls back like a rag doll. "And he said it was because I was his baby sister."

I vowed to find a way to help Octavia to a better life without adding more problems.

I felt the responsibility to help Velia and Octavia in any way I could. "I will talk to Paul when I get back to Patmos."

This became a heavy burden for my widowed, aging mother back in Patmos. But I would do my best as a family friend for this family that had rejected me as tutor because I happened to be a sixteen-year old woman seeking a man who would be slow to anger. And what they wanted focused on a boy that could inherit my family's generations of engineers, navigation inventors, and architects.

Kindness and peace in the home brings out a healthy glow and sweetness in any woman wherever she may be present. In a way, I felt responsible to do a good deed for Octavia and her mother. I feel now at a loss that

Velia succumbed, eaten by her resentment, and Octavia quickly had been signed away by Salonius, now years later, honored by miserly Cornelius's insistence of having Octavia's hand in marriage.

Some cannot help themselves. I thought about the striped silvery kitten. Nearly ten years had passed, and today I gazed fondly at the spitfire bride, Octavia, forged in the fires of her father's perpetual pool of anger, her mother's weak, hacking cough, persistent complaints of resentment, and growing frailty.

I'm back on Patmos with my friendly wolf-dog, far from Rome or Neapolis. I'm reading copies of Paul's letters, and he still savors the broth in my mother's sweet tavern and cares to gently pet the tavern's official greeter, our *canis-lupus,* protector of commitment to family, faith, and friends. With a dog in the home, there is harmony.

When in Rome, trust the volcano nearby as a better protector of Greek women than a slave rebellion on the loose. But here in Patmos, we sit in a circle and listen to Paul of Tarsus and those who follow. In this village we are welcome to freely question, seek answers, and think for ourselves. Our symbols, like our gears, are our *antikythera (from the Greek island of Antikythera long before we arrived on Patmos).* They stand for exploration by celestial navigation. Our destiny is beyond the stars.

Take the *"Sailing the Ancient Mediterranean with Paul of Patmos,*

Calliope, and a Friendly Dog, Xanthe"
Historical Creative Writing Assessment

∽ *Backstory and Clues:*

Are you best-suited to be a historical novelist, mystery writer, video or board game script writer/designer, short story sprinter, digital interactive story writer on ancient civilizations, a nonfiction writer, or an author of thrillers using historical settings or universal themes? Do you think like a fiction writer, investigative journalist, or an imaginative, creative nonfiction author writing biography in the style of genre or mainstream fiction?

How are you going to clarify and resolve the issues, problems, or situations in your plot by the way your characters behave to move the action forward? How do you get measurable results when writing fiction or creative nonfiction? Consider what steps you show to reveal how your story is resolved by the characters. This also is known as the dénouement.

Dénouement as it applies to a short story or novel is the final resolution. It's your clarification of a dramatic or narrative plot. What category of dénouement will your characters take to move the plot forward?

Take the writing style preference classifier and find out how you approach your favorite writing style using Toot's facts and acts. Which genre is for you--interactive, traditional, creative nonfiction, fiction, decisive or investigative?

Would you rather write for readers that need to interact with their own story endings or plot branches? Which style best fits you? What's your writing profile?

Enjoy this ancient echoes writing genre interest classifier and see the various ways in which way you can be more creative.

Do you prefer to write investigative, logical nonfiction or imaginative fiction—or a mixture of both? There are 35 questions—seven questions for each of the five pairs. There are 10 choices.

❖ *The 10 Choices:*

THE CHOICES:	
Grounded	Verve
Rational	Enthusiastic
Decisive	Investigative
Loner	Outgoing
Traditional	Change-Driven

Writer's Creativity Style Classifier

Creative (imaginative) writing (fiction or nonfiction) is about building and being remembered for what you build into your story, fractal by fractal and word by word. Civilizations are remembered for either what they build up or what they tear down. And your plot and story line can be the reason for their behaviors. Your characters can work for freedoms and equality for all, regardless of

tually were ancestors that designed and built the first *antikythera* device? (verve)

a. □

b. □

4. **Would you rather write about**

a. Calliope being chosen as a preferred and well-paid Greek tutor and companion for Velia's daughter, (enthusiastic) **or**

b. the mystery of why Calliope would have been chosen as one of the family slaves (if she couldn't prove with the correct scrolls) her Roman citizenship that had been awarded to her late father, known for his inventions, and all of his family in Patmos? (rational)?

    a. □

    b. □

5. **You are Calliope. Would you rather**

a. befriend Octavia and try to help her (enthusiastic) **or**

b. marry Cornelius or some other wealthy friend of Salonius in order to make sure your Roman citizenship was validated and you married into an aristocratic family, thereby assuring that you would never be enslaved and put to work as a tutor? (rational)

    a. □

    b. □

6. **As a writer following Octavia's life story from the age of five to adulthood as her companion, tutor, and nanny, would you rather**

a. create a laundry list of duties that she must learn as a child in a wealthy Roman family (down-to-earth) **or**

b. create a story where you, Calliope, and Octavia leave the house of Velia and Salonius to return to Patmos as female math enthusiasts teaching other women how to be financially independent as math and Greek tutors to the ancient Roman world (in the age of emperors)? (verve)

   a. ☐

   b. ☐

7. **Are you more interested in ending your story with**

a. Calliope marrying Cornelius or another wealthy friend or relative of Salonius in order to restore her family name as inventors from Patmos (decisive) **or**

b. would you rather let your story remain open for serialization, with Calliope running away to Alexandria with one of Velia's household slaves hiding from his Roman masters so he can restore his birthright as a Macedonian Prince? (investigative)

   a. ☐

   b. ☐

8. **If you were prince Calliope, would you prefer to**

a. decide to leave your own country to marry a famous Centurion because duty required it, knowing you'll probably be killed by someone from your native country when you become the wife of a famous Roman (decisive) **or**

b. stall for time as long as possible, waiting for validated information to arrive regarding the diplomatic climate between Greek artists, inventors, and engineers and Romans shipping Greek art, gold, and engineers to Rome without paying for the art/sculpture treasures? (investigative).

   a. ☐

   b. ☐

9. **You are Calliope, of Patmos. Would you**

a. speak in Greek in front of the Roman family that hired you to teach Greek to their daughter, thereby possibly inflaming the Roman patriotism in Salonius when you actually want to show your skill in teaching Salonius's daughter equally proficient in both Latin and Greek (investigative) **or**

b. plan and organize methodically to have a whole line of people from Patmos that are not household slaves close to you? (decisive)

   a. ☐

   b. ☐

10. Would you rather write about

a. terms of treaties between Greece and Rome when war with Carthage is the real issue (down-to-earth) **or**

b. problems with exports of figs and dates from Carthage in North Africa to Rome temporarily distract Roman rulers from plundering the art and sculpture of Greece? (verve)

a. □

b. □

11. Do you like writing about

a. enigmas set in motion by sea shells representing Venus rising from the ocean etched on intimate ancient Roman funerary equipment in a historical mystery novel (rational) **or**

b. why female mathematicians in ancient Rome and Greece were so often punished or martyred (enthusiastic)?

a. □

b. □

12. A *tag line* shows the mood/emotion in the voice--how a character speaks or acts. Are you more interested in

a. compiling, counting, and indexing *citations* or *quotes* from how-to books for writers (down-to-earth) **or**

b. compiling *tag lines* that explain in fiction dialogue the specific behaviors or gestures such as, "Yes, he replied timorously."? (verve)

　　a. □

　　b. □

13. Would you rather write

a. dialog (enthusiastic) **or**

b. description and narration? (rational)

　　a. □

　　b. □

14. To publicize your writing, would you rather

a. give spectacular presentations or shows without preparation or prior notice (investigative) **or**

b. have to prepare a long time in advance to speak or perform? (decisive)

　　a. □

　　b. □

15. If you were Calliope, would you prefer to

a. receive warnings well in advance and without surprises that Salonius is planning to make you a household slave? Salonius has hidden your Roman citizenship documents. Your late father owed him money. To solve your problem, you decide to team up with Velia's children, buy Salonius's household slaves with your widowed mother's inheritance.

Your mother sends you money in care of a retired Roman general loyal to your family in Patmos. You free Salonius's slaves and set sail for Patmos. The retired general has located proof of your family's right to claim a sum of money. You now have validation in the Roman world that your family's ancestors engineered the *antikythera* navigational device (decisive) **or**

b. adapt to last-moment changes by frequently having a new career in a new town. Your goal is to search your genealogy as you support yourself by planning lavish banquets for the rich and famous? (investigative)

    a. ☐

    b. ☐

16. As a tutor in ancient Rome would you

a. feel constrained by Salonius's time schedules and deadlines (due dates) (investigative) **or**

b. set realistic timetables and juggle priorities? (decisive)

    a. ☐

    b. ☐

math to demand that you greet and entertain her guests all evening at banquets.
(loner).

a. □

b. □

23. When Velia asks you to write love poems for her that she can hand to her secret lover, you

a. create the ideas for your poems by long discussions with Velia (outgoing) **or**

b. prefer to be alone when you reach deep down inside your spirit to listen before you tell her husband, Salonius. (loner)

    a. □

    b. □

24. You are searching your genealogy and prefer to

a. question different foreigners at boisterous celebrations in different languages (outgoing) **or**

b. disregard outside events and look at family inscriptions on the back of the *antikythera* device for family invention clues? (loner)

    a. □

    b. □

25. Velia asks you to develop ideas about how to test her daughter's lessons in front

of guests. You prefer to develop ideas through

a. reflection, meditation, and prayer (loner) **or**

b. discussions and interviews among Octavia's playmates on what makes Velia's daughter laugh. (outgoing)

    a. ☐

    b. ☐

26. As a young tutor to children, you are

a. rarely cautious about the family position of those with whom you socialize as long as they are kind, righteous people who do good deeds (outgoing) **or**

b. you are seeking one person with power to raise you from tutor who could at any moment become a slave, to owner of your own villa in Neapolis, if only others would pay you to ask your advice. (loner)

    a. ☐

    b. ☐

27. You are asked to take a Roman name while employed in the villa of Salonius and Velia instead of using your Greek name, Calliope. Would you

a. take a name that means 'remote' (loner) **or**

b. choose a special name for yourself that means, "She who shares time easily with many foreigners?" (outgoing)

a. □

b. □

28. Do you work better when you

a. spend your day off where no one can see you doing mathematics which societies in ancient Greece and Rome would never teach women to modulate (loner) **or**

b. spend your free time training teams of slave tutors to sculpt their masters' faces in clay when creating garden ceramics? (outgoing)

    a. □

    b. □

29. If you discovered a new land, would you build your cities upon

a. your wise elders' principles as they always have worked well before (traditional) **or**

b. unfamiliar cargo that traders brought from afar to civilize your land? (change-driven)

    a.□

    b.□

30. If you were an artist or scribe in ancient Rome, would you depict victories on a stone column exactly as

a. surviving witnesses from both sides recounted the events (change-driven) **or**

b. the way rulers from Rome want people to see how other civilizations live and look compared to Romans? (traditional)

a.☐

b.☐

31. Are you self-motivated? Would you avoid learning from Salonius and Velia, your masters, because

a. your masters don't keep up with the times (change-driven) **or**

b. your masters don't allow you to follow in your famous Greek ancestor's footsteps in design and engineering because you're a young woman or because you're a foreigner in Rome trying to get back your Roman citizenship papers? (traditional)

a.☐

b.☐

32. Would you prefer to

a. train tutors over and over the rest of your life because your father taught you how to do it well (traditional) **or**

b. move quickly from one project to another forever? (change-driven)

a.☐

b.☐

33. Do you feel like an outsider when

a. you think more about the future than about current chores (change-driven) **or**

b. invaders replace your Greek forefathers' familiar foods with less familiar Roman cuisine? (traditional)

a.☐

b.☐

34. Do you quickly

a. solve problems for those inside when you're coming from outside (change-driven) **or**

b. refuse to spend your treasures to develop new ideas that might fail? (traditional)

a.☐

b.☐

35. Would you rather listen to and learn from philosophers that

a. predict a future in which old habits are replaced with new ones (change-driven) **or**

b. are only interested in experiencing one day at a time? (traditional)

a.☐

b.☐

Self-Scoring the Test

Add up the number of answers for each of the following ten writing style traits for the 35 questions. There are seven questions for each group. The ten categories are made up of five opposite pairs.

Down-to-earth	**Verve**
Rational	**Enthusiastic**
Decisive	**Investigative**
Loner	**Outgoing**
Traditional	**Change-Driven**

Then put the numbers for each answer next to the categories. See the same self-scored test and results below.

1. Total Down-to-earth	6. Total Verve
2. Total Rational	7. Total Enthusiastic
3. Total Decisive	8. Total Investigative
4. Total Loner	9. Total Outgoing
5. Total Traditional	10. Total Change-Driven

To get your score, you're only adding up the number of answers for each of the 10 categories (five pairs) above. See the sample self-scored test below. Note that there are seven questions for each of the five pairs (or 10 designations). There are 35 questions. Seven questions times five categories equal 35 questions. Keep the number of questions you design for each category equal.

Here's a Sample Self-Scored Test

❧ *Take the "Sailing the Ancient Mediterranean with Paul of Patmos, Calliope, and Her Family's Dog, Xanthe" Creative Writing Assessment*

> Backstory and Clues: **Time Traveling the Ancient Mediterranean with Paul of Patmos, Calliope, and her Family's Dog, Xanthe**

❧ *Historical Fiction Creative Writing Assessment*

Are you best-suited to be a historical novelist, mystery writer, video or board game script writer/designer, short story sprinter, digital interactive story writer on ancient civilizations, a nonfiction writer, or an author of thrillers using historical settings or universal themes? Do you think like a fiction writer, investigative journalist, or an imaginative, creative nonfiction author writing biography in the style of genre or mainstream fiction?

How are you going to clarify and resolve the issues, problems, or situations in your plot by the way your characters behave to move the action forward? How do you get measurable results when writing fiction or creative nonfiction? Consider what steps you show to reveal how your story is resolved by the characters. This also is known as the d**énouement.**

Dénouement as it applies to a short story or novel is the final resolution. It's your clarification of a dramatic or narrative plot. What category of **dénouement** will your characters take to move the plot forward?

Take the writing style preference classifier and find out how you approach your favorite writing style using Toot's facts and acts. Which genre is for you--interactive, traditional, creative nonfiction, fiction, decisive or investigative?

Would you rather write for readers that need to interact with their own story endings or plot branches? Which style best fits you? What's your writing profile?

Enjoy this ancient echoes writing genre interest classifier and see the various ways in which way you can be more creative.

Do you prefer to write investigative, logical nonfiction or imaginative fiction—or a mixture of both? There are 35 questions—seven questions for each of the five pairs. There are 10 choices.

THE CHOICES:	
Grounded	Verve
Rational	Enthusiastic
Decisive	Investigative
Loner	Outgoing
Traditional	Change-Driven

Writer's Creativity Style Classifier

Creative (imaginative) writing (fiction or nonfiction) is about building and being remembered for what you build into your story, fractal by fractal and word by word. Civilizations are remembered for either what they build up or what they tear down. And your plot and story line can be the reason for their behaviors. Your characters can work for freedoms and equality for all, regardless of diversity, belief, or no belief, for unity, or for the right to remain nomadic or any other way you want them to be.

How do you want your story's characters and the plot (driven by characters) to be remembered by the world--by what they invent, create, or develop, or by what they implode, remove, or wipe out?

If a group of people are travelers or nomads, they can build stories from oral traditions out of seemingly "nothing" if the geographic areas they cover have no building materials such as trees or stone. Or art can be created on looms or from clay and minerals or from metals.

Creativity can be oral or artistic and can be told, recorded, or worn. You want your characters to be remembered for destroying a plague or disease or for building huge malls, enormous or useful architecture, or great centers of learning? Do you want your characters to be remembered for solving worldwide problems and getting measurable results? For providing detailed steps for others to follow? For moral and ethical revelations? Or as leaders and inventors? Or for taking humanity to newer planets? What is your goal as an imaginative writer? What are your preferences?

You are a **mystery writer** working on an interactive audio book of stories with clues for the Web about a scribe in ancient Rome and the Aegean Islands, who has unending adventures trying to track down the person who now owns the *antikytheria* device, a navigational gear tool and astronomical calendar for the

Mediterranean shipping trade that seems to be a type of ancient mechanical "computer" made of gears.

Your alter ego scribe and protagonist is in a race against time to save the 16-year old, Greek tutor, Calliope. She's an ingénue, who is the daughter of an inventor of navigational devices.

Calliope is about to be forced into slavery in the home of a wealthy but harsh ancient Roman family. The family is scared of the slave rebellions in Rome.

Calliope becomes the tutor and nanny/companion to that family's younger daughter. But Calliope is in danger of being forced into marriage with a friend of that family's patriarch, an older man named Cornelius, or harassed by the family's 20-year old son, or kept as a slave but required to work long hours as a tutor to the family's 5-year old daughter, Octavia.

Calliope's two goals are to find proof of her Roman citizenship to avoid being made a slave of the family where she lives as the tutor to their child and also to restore to her family the *antikythera* device stolen from her hands by Velia, the matriarch of the villa. She must also locate the correct scrolls that prove her late father's family line to be the true inventors and engineers of the much in demand and cherished navigational tool. Calliope must use her intelligence to solve her problems.

How will you write this interactive story, according to your writing style preferences? How will Calliope get back her family's newer addition to the *antikythera* invention based on an even more ancient Greek *antikythera* navigational device when it is taken away by Velia, the matriarch of the house?

✢ *Clues*

The leading character is 'Calliope,' the nanny, tutor, and scribe.

Calliope arrives with her status unknown as to whether she is the family's new slave, an employed tutor and nanny, or is to be adopted by the lady of the villa. Calliope is the daughter of a widow from Patmos, and Calliope's late father is descended from a family of inventors, architects, and engineers who have travelled the ancient Mediterranean from Patmos to Rome.

The Assessment

1. **To write your story, would you prefer to**

   a. go to the Greek archives of inventions now in ancient Rome in order to have translated two letters sent from Salonius to Calliope's late father, asking to send a tutor from Patmos to Rome for their five-year old daughter, Octavia (down-to-earth) **or**

   b. dig deeper and find out the connections between the proof of Roman citizenship for Calliope so she can avoid being made a slave and the proof of her father's lineage as inventors of the navigational device. (verve)

      a. □

      b. ■

2. **Would you be more interested in researching history and writing about**

a. the political and personal relationships that surfaced between the ancient Greeks and the Romans regarding Roman copying or taking of Greek sculpture and art works out of Greece to be placed in private Roman villas and public places (enthusiastic) **or**

b. analyze the business deals and diplomatic events between these equal powers to see who was winning the race to becoming the superpower of the century and whether the competition influenced Paul of Patmos's letters and writings to his Greek audiences? (rational)

a. ■

b. □

3. **Are you more interested in the fact that**

a. Calliope wrote all her letters in Latin, not in her native Greek (down-to-earth) **or**

b. Calliope would have to prove to Salonius and Velia that her late father's lineages actually were ancestors that designed and built the first *antikythera* device? (verve)

a. ■

b. □

4. 4. **Would you rather write about**

   a. Calliope being chosen as a preferred and well-paid Greek tutor and companion for Velia's daughter, (enthusiastic) **or**

   b. the mystery of why Calliope would have been chosen as one of the family slaves (if she couldn't prove with the correct scrolls) her Roman citizenship that had been awarded to her late father, known for his inventions, and all of his family in Patmos? (rational)?

      a. ■

      b. □

5. **You are Calliope. Would you rather**

   a. befriend Octavia and try to help her (enthusiastic) **or**

   b. marry Cornelius or some other wealthy friend of Salonius in order to make sure your Roman citizenship was validated and you married into an aristocratic family, thereby assuring that you would never be enslaved and put to work as a tutor? (rational)

      a. ■

      b. □

6. **As a writer following Octavia's life story from the age of five to adulthood as her**

companion, tutor, and nanny, would you rather

a. create a laundry list of duties that she must learn as a child in a wealthy Roman family (down-to-earth) **or**

b. create a story where you, Calliope, and Octavia leave the house of Velia and Salonius to return to Patmos as female math enthusiasts teaching other women how to be financially independent as math and Greek tutors to the ancient Roman world (in the age of emperors)? (verve)

   a. □

   b. ■

7. **Are you more interested in ending your story with**

a. Calliope marrying Cornelius or another wealthy friend or relative of Salonius in order to restore her family name as inventors from Patmos (decisive) **or**

b. would you rather let your story remain open for serialization, with Calliope running away to Alexandria with one of Velia's household slaves hiding from his Roman masters so he can restore his birthright as a Macedonian Prince? (investigative)

   a. □

   b. ■

8. **If you were prince Calliope, would you prefer to**

a. decide to leave your own country to marry a famous Centurion because duty required it, knowing you'll probably be killed by someone from your native country when you become the wife of a famous Roman (decisive) **or**

b. stall for time as long as possible, waiting for validated information to arrive regarding the diplomatic climate between Greek artists, inventors, and engineers and Romans shipping Greek art, gold, and engineers to Rome without paying for the art/sculpture treasures? (investigative).

    a. ☐
    b. ■

9. **You are Calliope, of Patmos. Would you**

a. speak in Greek in front of the Roman family that hired you to teach Greek to their daughter, thereby possibly inflaming the Roman patriotism in Salonius when you actually want to show your skill in teaching Salonius's daughter equally proficient in both Latin and Greek (investigative) **or**

b. plan and organize methodically to have a whole line of people from Patmos that are not household slaves close to you? (decisive)

    a. ■
    b. ☐

10. Would you rather write about

a. terms of treaties between Greece and Rome when war with Carthage is the real issue (down-to-earth) **or**

b. problems with exports of figs and dates from Carthage in North Africa to Rome temporarily distract Roman rulers from plundering the art and sculpture of Greece? (verve)

    a. □

    b. ■

11. Do you like writing about

a. enigmas set in motion by sea shells representing Venus rising from the ocean etched on intimate ancient Roman funerary equipment in a historical mystery novel (rational) **or**

b. why female mathematicians in ancient Rome and Greece were so often punished or martyred (enthusiastic)?

    a. □

    b. ■

12. A *tag line* shows the mood/emotion in the voice--how a character speaks or acts. Are you more interested in

a. compiling, counting, and indexing *citations* or *quotes* from how-to books for writers (down-to-earth) **or**

b. compiling *tag lines* that explain in fiction dialogue the specific behaviors or gestures such as, "Yes, he replied timorously."? (verve)

a. □

b. ■

13. Would you rather write

a. dialog (enthusiastic) **or**

b. description and narration? (rational)

a. ■

b. □

14. To publicize your writing, would you rather

a. give spectacular presentations or shows without preparation or prior notice (investigative) **or**

b. have to prepare a long time in advance to speak or perform? (decisive)

a. ■

b. □

15. If you were Calliope, would you prefer to

a. receive warnings well in advance and without surprises that Salonius is planning to make you a household slave? Salonius has hidden your Roman citizenship documents. Your late father owed him money. To solve your problem, you decide to team up with Velia's children, buy Salonius's household slaves with your widowed mother's inheritance.

Your mother sends you money in care of a retired Roman general loyal to your family in Patmos. You free Salonius's slaves and set sail for Patmos. The retired general has located proof of your family's right to claim a sum of money. You now have validation in the Roman world that your family's ancestors engineered the *antikythera* navigational device (decisive) **or**

b. adapt to last-moment changes by frequently having a new career in a new town. Your goal is to search your genealogy as you support yourself by planning lavish banquets for the rich and famous? (investigative)

    a. □

    b. ■

16. As a tutor in ancient Rome would you

a. feel constrained by Salonius's time schedules and deadlines (due dates) (investigative) **or**

b. set realistic timetables and juggle priorities? (decisive)

    a. ■

    b. □

17. **As a family friend of Paul of Patmos, do you feel bound to**

  a. go with social custom in Rome, do the activities itemized on the social calendar, and not rise above your station (decisive) **or**

  b. make no commitments or assumptions about what's the right thing to do because time changes plans? (investigative)

     a. ☐

     b. ■

18. **In your letter to Salonius and Velia about what you want to do with your future now that you are sixteen, would you write**

  a. one brief, concise, and to the point letter (rational) **or**

  b. one sociable, friendly, empathetic and time-consuming letter? (enthusiastic)

     a. ☐

     b. ■

19. **To decide how you can help little Octavia, would you make a list of**

  a. the pros and cons of each person close to you (rational) **or**

  b. varied comments and dialogue overheard from friends or relatives on what they say behind your back regarding how you influence them and what they want from you? (enthusiastic)

a. □

b. ■

20. Would you rather investigate

a. the detailed facts about Salonius and Velia (down-to-earth) **or**

b. want to study the big picture of the entire household? (verve)

a. □

b. ■

21. You're a tutor/nanny who

a. seldom makes errors of detail when looking for clues such as taking notice of Velia's present to Salonius—a bowl of mushrooms and a feather dipped in an emetic. (down-to-earth) **or**

b. prefer writing secret love poems to Salonius's dinner guest disguised as prayers to a garden statue of Minerva. (verve)

a. □

b. ■

22. As a tutor in ancient Rome, you become

a. tired when you teach all day in a breezy atrium (outgoing) **or**

b. tired when Velia interrupts your concentration on teaching Octavia languages and math to demand that you greet and entertain her guests all evening at banquets. (loner).

a. □

b. ■

23. **When Velia asks you to write love poems for her that she can hand to her secret lover, you**

a. create the ideas for your poems by long discussions with Velia (outgoing) **or**

b. prefer to be alone when you reach deep down inside your spirit to listen before you tell her husband, Salonius. (loner)

a. □

b. ■

24. **You are searching your genealogy and prefer to**

a. question different foreigners at boisterous celebrations in different languages (outgoing) **or**

b. disregard outside events and look at family inscriptions on the back of the *antikythera* device for family invention clues? (loner)

a. □

b. ■

25. Velia asks you to develop ideas about how to test her daughter's lessons in front of guests. You prefer to develop ideas through

a. reflection, meditation, and prayer (loner) **or**

b. discussions and interviews among Octavia's playmates on what makes Velia's daughter laugh. (outgoing)

a. ■

b. □

26. As a young tutor to children, you are

a. rarely cautious about the family position of those with whom you socialize as long as they are kind, righteous people who do good deeds (outgoing) **or**

b. you are seeking one person with power to raise you from tutor who could at any moment become a slave, to owner of your own villa in Neapolis, if only others would pay you to ask your advice. (loner)

a. □

b. ■

27. You are asked to take a Roman name while employed in the villa of Salonius and Velia instead of using your Greek name, Calliope. Would you

a. take a name that means 'remote' (loner) **or**

b. choose a special name for yourself that means, "She who shares time easily with many foreigners?" (outgoing)

a. □

b. ■

28. Do you work better when you

a. spend your day off where no one can see you doing mathematics which societies in ancient Greece and Rome would never teach women to modulate (loner) **or**

b. spend your free time training teams of slave tutors to sculpt their masters' faces in clay when creating garden ceramics? (outgoing)

a. ■

b. □

29. If you discovered a new land, would you build your cities upon

a. your wise elders' principles as they always have worked well before (traditional) **or**

b. unfamiliar cargo that traders brought from afar to civilize your land? (change-driven)

a.□

b. ■

30. If you were an artist or scribe in ancient Rome, would you depict victories on a stone column exactly as

a. surviving witnesses from both sides re-counted the events (change-driven) **or**

b. the way rulers from Rome want people to see how other civilizations live and look compared to Romans? (traditional)

a. ■

b.□

31. Are you self-motivated? Would you avoid learning from Salonius and Velia, your masters, because

a. your masters don't keep up with the times (change-driven) **or**

b. your masters don't allow you to follow in your famous Greek ancestor's footsteps in design and engineering because you're a young woman or because you're a foreigner in Rome trying to get back your Roman citizenship papers? (traditional)

a. ■

b.□

32. Would you prefer to

a. train tutors over and over the rest of your life because your father taught you how to do it well (traditional) **or**

b. move quickly from one project to another forever? (change-driven)

a. □

b. ■

33. Do you feel like an outsider when

a. you think more about the future than about current chores (change-driven) **or**

b. invaders replace your Greek forefathers' familiar foods with less familiar Roman cuisine? (traditional)

a. ■

b.□

34. Do you quickly

a. solve problems for those inside when you're coming from outside (change-driven) **or**

b. refuse to spend your treasures to develop new ideas that might fail? (traditional)

a. ■

b.□

35. Would you rather listen to and learn from philosophers that

a. predict a future in which old habits are replaced with new ones (change-driven) **or**

b. are only interested in experiencing one day at a time? (traditional)

a.□

b. ■

⤳ Scores

Total Down-to-earth	0	Total Verve	5
Total Rational	0	Total Enthusiastic	7
Total Decisive	0	Total Investigative	7
Total Loner	4	Total Outgoing	3
Total Traditional	2	Total Change-Driven	5

The four highest numbers of answers are enthusiastic, investigative, imaginative loner. Choose the highest numbers first as having the most importance (or weight) in your writing style preference. Therefore, your own *creative writing* **style** *and the way you plot your character's actions, interests, and goals* (for fiction writing and specifically mystery writing) is an **enthusiastic investigative vivacious (verve-with-imagination) loner. Your five personality letters would be: E I V L C.** (Scramble the letters to make a word to remember, the name Clive, in this case.)

Note that there is a tie between C and V. Both have a score of '5'. However, since 'V' (verve) which signifies vivacious imagination with gusto competes with 'C', being change-driven, the 'verve' in the vivacious personality wracked with creative imagination would wither in a traditional corporation that emphasizes routinely running a tight ship. Traditional firms seek to imitate successful corporations of the past that worked well and still work. They don't need to be fixed often unless they make noise.

Instead, the dominantly change-driven creative individual would flourish better with a forward-looking, trend-setting creative corporation and build security from flexibility of job skill. When in doubt, turn to action verbs to communicate your 'drive.' If you're misplaced, you won't connect as well with co-workers and may be dubbed "a loose cannon."

You know you're writing in the right genre when your personality connects with the genre of fiction or creative nonfiction readers and groups to share meaning. Communication is the best indicator of your personality matching a novel's main character traits with readers. It's all about connecting more easily with readers similar to your preferences.

Your main character or alter-ego could probably be an enthusiastic investigative imaginative loner. But you'd not only have lots of imagination and creativity—but also verve, that vivacious gusto. You'd have fervor, dash, and élan.

The easily excitable, investigative, creative/imaginative loner described as having verve, is more likely to represent what you feel inside your core personality, your self-insight, as you explore your own values and interests.

It's what you feel like, what your *values* represent on this test at this moment in time. That's how a lot of personality tests work. This one is customized for fiction writers. Another test could be tailored for career area interests or for analyzing what stresses you. Think of your personality as your virtues.

Qualities on this customized test that are inherent in the test taker who projects his or her values and personality traits onto the characters would represent more of a sentimental, charismatic, imaginative, investigative individual who likes to work alone most of the time.

The person could at times be more change-driven than traditional. The real test is whether the test taker is consistent about these traits or values on many different assessments of interests, personality, or values.

What's being tested here is imaginative fiction writing style. Writing has a personality, genre, or character of its own. The writing style and values are revealed in the way the characters drive the plot.

These sample test scores measure the preference, interest, and trait of the writer. The tone and mood are measured in this test. It's a way of sharing meaning, of communicating by driving the characters and the plot in a selected direction.

This assessment 'score' reveals a fiction writer who is enthusiastically investigative in tone, mood, and texture. These 'traits' or values apply to the writer as well as to the primary characters in the story.

The traits driving a writer's creativity also drive the main characters. Writer and characters work in a partnership of alter egos to move the plot forward. A creativity test lets you select and express the action, attitudes, and values of the story in a world that you shape according to clues, critical thinking, and personal likes.

PART VI

How to Write a Novel/ Story/Script by Developing Depth of Character that Drives the Plot of Your Fiction

Shallow, cardboard characters driven by unbelievable plots are gone. What sells currently in fiction is depth of character's personalities, commitment, and plots about making ancient roots contemporary. Mainstream novels and thrillers are in.

The goal of today's manuscript doctor in fiction writing is to help writers avoid pitfalls that blindside your story's protagonist and could derail your manuscript. Instead of presenting your story's characters with shallow, stick-figure personalities, develop depth.

Start by slowly revealing growth, step-by-step. First your protagonist transcends past mistakes, bad decisions, and immature choices. Then he or she forgives and moves on to share confidence with others. Editors want to hear resilient voices rising in fiction dialog. Ethnography is in with mainstream fiction.

Here are the steps to take. Your main character, called the protagonist in your story, novel, or drama, gains depth through self-scrutiny. Editors need a system by which to judge your salable fiction. That system depends on the measured range of change of your main characters.

They derive that system from the simplest words describing your character's behavior found right in front of you, in your dictionary and thesaurus.

Divide your short story into three parts. Instead of calling those parts the beginning, middle, and end as you learned in literature classes, call your three parts foresight, insight, and hindsight.

✦ Foresight

You show growth by taking a proverb and/or a quotation containing universal values and flesh it out—grow it like you grow crystals in a chemistry set. As you stretch out your proverb, fleshing it out as dialog and description, you will have set up the first part of your story, the beginning, or more precisely the foresight stage. It's about knowing growth will occur and having to make a choice about which path to take. You'll find plenty of proverbs in the Bible, in a published book of proverbs, or in a book of famous quotations from history.

✧ Insight

The middle of your story is the insight stage. Ordinary people, including peers, colleagues, and neighbors making general conversation across lawns are responsible for words describing behavior, emotions, and personality traits. Those descriptions and observations end up in novels and thesauri.

Authors look at descriptions of behaviors or emotions, attitudes, and moods in dictionaries or thesauri. When you're looking for just the right word the dictionary is the prime source of definitions of personality preferences.

Then you look at proverbs to flesh out into a story focusing on the behavior traits of the specific personality type you want to target. That's one way you develop depth in a character in a work of fiction.

The other way is through inspiration and observation of real people in your environment that you fictionalize using as much accurate historical backgrounds as you can to make your fiction believable. If your fiction is believable it will hold attention better, even in a fantasy novel set in the far future or past. An example is "Star Wars" or "Valley of the Horses."

↤ Hindsight

If your main character had one lesson to learn in life, what would it be? Your characters should reveal their personality traits through their behavior and actions. Let the character's personality unfold by example. Use simple words for dialog--words found in most dictionaries.

The gestures, patterns, and actions define behavior more than the words.

Emotion is shown by *tag lines*. These lines reveal the character's attitude when any words are spoken. Tag lines prevent miscommunication. You can say, "He took a sudden interest in his shoes." But if you

say, "He's shy." The word 'shy' is too abstract to define the behavior. You need to show what shyness looks like in one sentence. It's your pitch for your character in one line of action that presents the big picture of the protagonist's personality traits.

Your plot can be summed up in a proverb. Pick a proverb that is close to the theme or plot of your story. Then expand the proverb with dialog and actions. Describe surroundings.

Use action verbs, and adjectives for character, personality, attitude, and mood. Narrow your descriptive, behavioral "tag words" and tag lines to fourteen opposite concepts: *feet on the ground or head in the clouds; sentimental or rational; traditional or change-oriented; decisive or explorative; impatient or patient; investigative or trusting; loner; or outgoing.*

Use action verbs to describe behavior or production, words such as designed, wrote, played, worked, or shopped. For inspiration, see my book on action verbs for communicators titled, *801 Action Verbs for*

221

Communicators: Position Yourself First with Action Verbs for Journalists, Speakers, Educators, Students, Resume-Writers, Editors, ISBN : 0595319114.

Before you write fiction, you need to define the behavior and personality of each main character, especially your protagonist and antagonist.

Those vernacular words from around the world end up in dictionaries and thesaurus, often translated into English language dictionaries, and most often focusing on a variety of personality aspects. These definitions help me design tests. Use the vernacular to get the big picture of your protagonist's and antagonist's personalities. They should be opposite in personality and equal in strength. Don't take away their choices.

From the dictionary, make a list of personality traits and businesses that reflect the personalities of their owners. To get a handle on your main character's personality, break down conversation to the simplest parts of speech. Use descriptive words to describe the decisions your characters make.

Even water cooler gossip is a good source of listening to descriptive words that describe behavior or a company's mission.

Describe personality traits by painting visual portraits with the simplest possible of definitions of behavior described by specific words. Listen to the emphasis people put on certain words. Does your character say one word marvelously or timorously?

What words are in your thesaurus describing a personality trait, style, attribute, mood, texture, or preference? How do dictionaries describe one aspect of personality, behavior, preference, or attitude? Is it based on observation by average people making casual conversation?

The more words you find in a dictionary describing how people talk or act or present their attitudes, the more important in that society a particular aspect of character is to the specific society and language. If you have writer's block, look at synonyms and antonyms and match them to your favorite proverb. Can they describe an anecdote?

Start your story with a 1,500 word vignette or anecdote and keep expanding the action as the characters' personalities drive the action forward and expand the events and their response to the events. Do they act or react to events or other people they meet or observe? Dictionaries contain the simplest definitions of human behavior described by people gossiping.

Simplicity in a novel, drama, or story means the story plot and actions of the main characters give you all the answers you were looking for in your life in exotic places, but found it close by. Your novel sells when it poses the least financial risk to the publisher.

Don't make up characters and sub-plots that are too complex for the average reader to understand and get the big picture with one reading. Emphasize simplicity.

Simplicity in a novel usually means the protagonist gets to stand on his or her two feet and put bread on the table because of commitment to family, faith, or friends. The salable novel or story has a moral point containing universal values that it is only right to pull your own weight and care for others, repair the world, and give charity while making your village or homestead a kinder and gentler place.

into your story or novel to validate concepts of what sold well in the past—a best seller. Remember that your book is salable only so much as it poses the least financial risk to the publisher. Avoid tautology when writing dialog. The kiss of death is to have the characters speak about the same idea using different words throughout the manuscript.

The editor is looking for a tangible product rather than an intangible idea to sell to readers. Your characters must show confidence and have their own voices of resilience. Usually if you write one novel and sell it to a publisher, you get a contract to write two to four more to make it a trilogy or a series of five novels . The publisher wants to see endurance in you and in each of your characters if you are assigned a contract to write three to five more novels.

Editors want to see how each character makes sense of his or her world in your fiction. How reliable are you to write a series of novels or stories on the same theme, perhaps using the same characters? How reliable are the characters in your fiction to come up with a series of stories or novels using the same characters set in the same era with different plots?

What's selling now in mainstream fiction? Growing in popularity are sagas and novels of deep ancestry. Because of the human genome project and the popularity of DNA-driven genealogy, novels set against a background of *phylogeography* and exploration are becoming popular, as in the mainstream novel with a hint of romantic suspense and the time countdown pacing of a thriller titled, *The DNA Detectives: Working Against Time.*

You might wish to look at the new tools that complement the evidence of the past in a novel set in contemporary times. Novels and tales about how we decipher the details carried in our genes open literary doors. Combine fiction with science written simply as a gripping story.

How to Write a Historical Novel Weaving Characters with Depth

Historical novels have a beginning, middle, and end like all stories and dramas. They also need a platform—visible expertise. But how the beginning, middle, and end are divided up and equally balanced in the planning stage may determine whether your novel will be salable to most mainstream publishers.

There's a precise but hidden formula for planning, organizing, and writing salable historical novels. The formula applies only if you're writing for most mainstream publishers of popular historical fiction. Publishers can change and vary their requirements.

So check with them before you write anything. You can find a list of publishers of historical fiction in most listings of writers' markets either online or in book and magazine listings.

Begin with your public or university librarian to make a list of 50 publishers of historical fiction that you will query. When you get a go-ahead to send your manuscript or an outline and sample chapters from the publisher, here's how to start your plan before your even begin to write your fiction proposal.

Many publishers do not require an agent. If you contact those requiring an agent, you can send the fiction proposal, three sample chapters, and an outline of your plan.

To begin actually writing an historical novel, begin first with the dialog as if you were writing a radio or stage play. Instead of writing in camera angles or lighting or sound effects, you'll fill in your description. Use dialog as the framework or skeleton of your historical novel.

Then build your action scenes around the dialogue with description and tag lines. You use tag lines to describe body gestures, emotional mood, and behavior. Tag lines are used in novels and stories to let the reader know the character's attitude and tone of voice.

For example, you can say he sniffed the roast, but you won't know what he thought of the roast unless you add a tag line in your dialogue such as, "Joe sashayed into the restaurant at closing time, sniffed the roast plangently, and wailed a mournful sound of delight like the breaking of waves." Now you know how he felt as he smelled the food in the restaurant.

Genres of Historical Fiction

The six genres within historical fiction divide into social history, exploration-adventure, biography, intrigue-suspense, sagas, and historical romance. Children's, women's, specific age group appeal novels including young adult's historical fiction also fall into these six genres, including family sagas spanning generations. In young adult fiction, the word length usually runs about 40,000 words. The appropriate page count of the usual adult historical fiction tome may run 75,000 to 100,000 words. Young adult family sagas are shorter in word length, about half the size of adult historical family or adventure sagas.

Biographical fiction runs from 50,000 to 70,000 words. And historical suspense, thrillers, or mystery tomes run about 60,000 words. Historical sagas set in ancient or medieval times can run 100,000 to 120,000 words, depending upon what word count the publisher prefers and can afford to publish. Historical fantasy is another category that falls under the fantasy fiction genre rather than historical fiction which usually is based on social history.

Dividing the Twenty-Four Chapters of a Historical Novel into Push and Pull of Conflict

Historical novels are divided into 12 chapters of dialog and description that push the plot forward and 12 chapters of dialog and description that pull the tension and conflict backwards. The even-numbered chapters create more problems to solve and additional growth and change for your main characters.

Even-numbered chapters show results that can be measured in each character's inner growth, reflection, emotions, dialog, behavior, frame of mind, mood, attitude, tag lines, and arc of change. Odd-numbered chapters are devoted to descriptions of locations, dates and times, geography, folklore, customs, habits, ethnology, nuances, settings, ceremonies, adventure, explorations, coming of age rituals, travel, descriptions of village life, cooking, costumes, warfare, military and social history backgrounds. For every action in a historical novel, there's that old cliché, "the equal and opposite reaction."

The Twelve Even-Numbered Chapters

Divide your historical novel into 24 chapters. Number those chapters on your outline and plan. Next separate 12 even-numbered chapters from the 12 odd-numbered. On the even numbered chapters write your character's dialog showing the rise of dramatic tension, the conflict, the push-and pull of any relationships or romance.

Your characters in a historical novel need to solve a problem and show the reader the results, the range of change, and their inner growth. What protagonists think of themselves in their social history context are shown in the even chapters. How they act toward others showing how they have grown by the midpoint of your story and finally by the ending chapter belongs in the 12 even-numbered chapters.

Write your character's dialog within the even-numbered chapters showing descriptions, locations, settings, scenes, action, adventure, and exotic descriptions of ceremonies, rituals, and significant life story highlights or turning points and events that animate your writing—make the writing come alive with sparkle, charisma, and the dash of adventure.

The Twelve Odd-Numbered Chapters

If you're writing an historical thriller, the odd-numbered pages get the physical action such as the ticking clock or count down to the high point of your novel. In historical mysteries, thrillers, and intrigue, the ticking clock is more like a ticking bomb.

Time evaporates at a faster and faster rate the farther you read into the book. The pace speeds up dramatically using more conflict and action where the characters need speedier reaction times with each advancing chapter as you head toward the middle point of your story.

Let the characters drive your plot forward. That's how you illustrate the illusion of the count-down and create the push and pull tension in a historical novel.

It's the same technique used in a thriller, without the historical attributes, settings, and costume drama or historical dialects and props, such as a setting at Versailles in the 18th century. Historical novels portray character-driven plots.

Begin Your First Chapter by Writing the Dialog

Your first chapter—chapter one—is an odd-numbered chapter. Here's the chapter where you put your setting, props, and descriptions. You're staring at a blank page. What do you write as your first sentence? Ask yourself what is your main character's payoff or reward in the book?

Is his or her reward to understand and control nature in order to become rich and powerful, run away from unbearable duty, get recognition, be remembered, and make an impact, or be loved and also be the center of attention?

You can break down your protagonist's goal or life purpose into four categories: control, duty, attention, and impact. To avoid writer's block on that blank first page, you write 90 seconds of dialog. Read it in 90 seconds aloud to a digital recorder. Play it back. How smooth does it sound to your ears?

Do real people talk that way? Is your setting and dialog believable?

After the first line of dialog, put in some of your background settings, dates, geography, action, and other props belonging in the odd-numbered chapters. Start a conversation between two characters. Then have them answer the questions or pose a new question by the end of the first page. Don't crowd everything that's important onto the first page.

Introduce your novel a little at a time to readers. Don't give the whole story away in the first chapter. In your outline, put in chapter summaries and headlines, not the whole story. Put your plan down after the first chapter.

Never start a historical novel with people in transit. Begin when they arrive at their new destination or write a historical novel that takes place entirely on the ship and end it when they step off the plank at their destination.

After you have your first page of dialogue written, insert in between the dialog the descriptions of geography, location, dates, foods, costumes, room descriptions, and anything else you will be putting into your odd chapters, usually falling on the right side of the book pages.

That's where the right eye travels first in a right-handed person. Then you write the first chapter as if it were act one of a 24-minute play, but don't put in any stage directions or sound effects. In fact, each of your chapters can total 24 pages. You're aiming for balance. Beware of short and long chapters in an historical novel or any story or drama.

Keep in mind attention span. The average attention span of a reader is seven minutes, same as the attention span for viewing video.

That's why commercials are inserted at every 10 minute break. The human brain needs a pause every 90 seconds to recharge. Knowing those elements of time, keep your scene segments changing every seven minutes and pausing for a change every 90 seconds of average reading time. Usually it takes a minute to read one page.

Your entire book would be 24 chapters. So keep the number 24 in mind as your yardstick. The pages don't have to be exact, of course, but you need to balance your chapters so that one chapter is not much longer than any other.

Instead, you describe in animated language, the geographic setting and the century or date. Animated language is written by using action verbs—designed, wrote, built, cured, vaccinated, or fired or ....as in "The charivari and consonance of healing frequencies fired from the klaxon's usual noise."

Avoid Tautology

Animate historical writing by avoiding tautology which means: don't repeat the same ideas using different words. How many words a publisher wants varies with each publisher. It costs less to publish a 50,000 word book than a book twice that size. Historical young adult novels run about 40,000 words. Historical novels can be family sagas that read as if they were talking maps and family atlases.

Begin your planning stage of your outline by first compiling your plot and the names of your character, dates, customs, ethnography, social history, biography, and folklore in a computer file folder. Keep at least two backup copies on CDs and also printed out on paper in case your computer crashes or your files are lost.

Buy a 3-ring loose leaf notebook for your paper copies. In the binder place all materials related to your book in progress. When the book is published, you'll need a second loose leaf notebook binder to keep track of publicity, press releases, reviews, contracts, and correspondence from your publisher and from the media. Place those little one-inch binder insert covers or tabs to label each chapter of your book.

Don't leave your book on the screen. Print out each chapter to edit and revise in the loose leaf note book. Put the book's title on the spine. Put into your note book plastic inserts.

Attach a tab to label your notes on research for historical accuracy. Put another tab for your synopsis, plan, outline, summarized chapters with chapter headings, and other notes. In another loose leaf notebook after the book is published, do the same type of labeling with plastic inserts and tabs for your editing, contracts, reviews, promotions, publicity press interviews, spinoff articles, history fact-checking, and royalty notices.

Keep your two notebooks in a metal filing cabinet, and keep copies of the same in your computer. One format will back up the other format. If your computer fails, you have everything printed out on paper and two or three CD copies of everything in a fire-proof metal filing cabinet

or box. When your editor calls, you can find anything in moments if you label your chapters and other materials and keep them close by.

After your book is published your second notebook will track royalties, reviews, the book cover design information or ideas, editing/revisions, query letters, and research of your potential market of readers or age groups and ethnic associations interested in the historical novel.

Historical novels are about looking for answers to solve problems and get results in exotic places, but finding simple answers were right under your fingers. You want to emphasize universal values such as commitment to family and friends, caring for one another, repairing social ills and sickness, earning a living and becoming independent, supporting your children and keeping the family together against all odds, or finding freedom, faith and values, in the virtues of finding and being accepted a new home land.

Another genre in historical fiction is the family saga. The saga may be fictionalized but it reads like biography. Fictional sagas use action verbs in the dialogue. They read almost like a drama. And the action verbs animate the writing. The opposite of animated writing is flat writing, where passive verbs weaken the story. Historical novels become weaker when the plot drives the characters.

The characters should drive the plot faster and faster to a conclusion where problems are solved or conflicts resolved. You have closure at the end for the characters. Or they transcend past mistakes and rise above them. The last chapter gives the characters a type of choice and balance they did not have at the beginning of the book. The characters grow.

They change with the times and inspire the reader. Or they are heroes because of sticking to their purpose and commitment.

The protagonists don't abandon their family or friends. But if they make mistakes, they find closure in rising above the mistakes by seeing more possibilities in the simple answers instead of the complex ones. Simplicity of answers close by is the formula for the historical novel that emphasizes growth and change for the better.

Before you write your plan, make a map or family atlas of your characters and summarize their problems and personalities in two paragraphs. Draw them on a map and point to how they relate to or interact with other characters and how they influence the other characters and the results. Read the book title, *Silk Stockings Glimpses of 1904 Broadway,* or *A 19th Century Immigrant's Love Story.* It shows how a love story intertwines with a historical novel that can be both a social history, romance novel, and historical novel or family saga rolled into one published book.

Write Two Scenes for Each Chapter

Your first chapter will consist of two scenes. Write those two scenes before sending them out to a publisher in an outline which usually asks for three sample chapters and an outline summary of one chapter (summarized by two paragraphs) for each of the 24 chapters of your book. Almost all mainstream novels consist of two scenes per chapter. Take apart any mainstream novel, and you'll see those two distinctive scenes in each chapter.

Within each chapter you'll have one scene of interaction between two characters or a character and his or her family and one action scene. So keep this formula in mind: one relationship scene and one action scene. It has been said by published authors in the past decade and

236

repeated at talks and seminars where published authors speak to other authors repeating this formula.

When you first plan your historical novel, separate the relationship side from the action side. First summarize the relationship side and then do the same for the action side. Then bring both together in one chapter. In every relationship scene and in every action scene, you will have your characters interacting together.

You need to make a laundry list in your plan of what happens specifically on the relationship side. Then in your odd-numbered chapters, you will fill in the plot side, the mystery side, the action side, the geography, costume, food, ethnography, travel and ballroom or battlefield side.

What you don't want to do is have all even-numbered chapters where characters do nothing but talk or all odd-numbered chapters where characters don't speak to each other and just travel the roads or sail the seas or fight the wars. No, that's just the way you outline your plan, your skeleton. Now you bring the relationship scenes together and the action scenes together and put them interplaying in each chapter. At this point, you'll start writing your book. In the actual book, the reader will not see a difference between the odd and even chapters.

It's in your planning stage that you separate each set of 12 chapters totaling 24 chapters. So when you finally bring the chapters together to weave them slowly, what you have left is an historical mainstream novel with "two scenes per chapter, one relationship scene and one action scene," as it has been said by numerous published authors speaking at writer's seminars or meetings.

The quote I heard most often from popular published novelists emphasized that "Your protagonists interact together in the relationship and action scenes." What you do plan for in your historical mainstream novel is writing 24 chapters.

Your first step is to write up a plan that shows chapter by chapter exactly what is happening, changing, and moving the plot forward on the relationship side and on the plot or action side. Then you have to balance relationship and dialogue against plot or action. When the two sides are in balance as if on a seesaw, you have a salable historical mainstream novel.

In your plan, you'd have two columns, one for scenes with relationships showing communication, connection, and interaction using dialog. And in your other column, you'd describe your plot using scenes depicting action and adventure.

This is the best way to organize your novel before you sit down to write. It's set up so you can get a handle on what you're doing and find any scene or chapter quickly to do fact checking with actual historical events.

When you've picked apart your book's main points, results, and are able to show how the characters solved problems leading to growth and change, commitment, closure, or transcending past choices and taking alternative paths, you have arrived at a point in organization where every turning point or significant event and relationship or social history highlight is labeled and filed. Now that you have organized the details, it's time to flesh out your story.

Historical Novels Spring from the Universal Message in Proverbs

Where do you get your storyline? You begin with a proverb related to the history your depicting. Look at a book of proverbs. Choose one. Flesh out the proverb into a story. Take a course in storytelling or read a book on how to be a storyteller.

Note most fairy tales and historical stories are built around proverbs with ageless, universal values and truths or are related to a culture's folklore and history. You can also use a proverb from the Bible or from any other similar book of any religion. Use an indigenous culture's proverbs or those from ancient cultures or hidden histories. You can write a historical novel about military dog, cat, or horse heroes.

Your story line can come out of a proverb or familiar quotation based on still older proverbs of any culture. If you need a plot, a proverb is the first place to look for inspiration or a start. Many novelists use proverbs as inspiration to write one-sentence pitch lines for their novels.

Before you write anything, summarize the pitch line of your book in one sentence. Pretend you were selling your novel to a movie producer. Pitch the book in ten seconds or less using one sentence. Here's one example used many times in lectures by scriptwriting course professors, "*Star Trek is Wagon Train in outer space.*" Perhaps your historical novel resembles various popular cultures placed in a new context.

About the Author

ANNE HART is a popular, independent behavioral science journalist, and author of 90+ published paperback books related to instruction in the craft of writing, creativity, and memory enhancement. Since June 17, 1959, Anne Hart, specializing in creativity enhancement studies, has been writing articles, novels, short stories, plays, poems, how-to books, creative nonfiction, and essays and holds a graduate degree in English/creative writing-fiction emphasis.

Hart writes books, stories, and/or articles on DNA-driven genealogy, nutritional genomics, and epigenetic-related topics. She writes freelance for various age groups, including dog stories with happy endings for all holidays for readers aged 12-17 and their families. This author also writes instructional materials and articles on how to write salable short stories and novels.

She is a member of the American Society of Journalists and Mensa. Her books in print are listed on her Web site at http://annehart.tripod.com. Anne Hart's goal is to research how creative writing, music, and art merge and can be applied as healing and creativity enhancement tools.

Also see this author's book titled, **Who's Buying Which Popular Short Fiction Now, & What Are They Paying?** And enjoy the novel and story book: **Dogs with Careers: Ten Happy-Ending Stories of Purpose and Passion** which also features the animation script titled, "Zyzyx, the flying Labrador retriever."

Paperback Books Currently in Print Written by Anne Hart

1. 101+ Practical Ways to Raise Funds: A Step-by-Step Guide with Answers

2. 101 Ways to Find Six-Figure Medical or Popular Ghostwriting Jobs & Clients

3. 102 Ways to Apply Career Training in Family History/Genealogy

4. 1700 Ways to Earn Free Book Publicity

5. 30+ Brain-Exercising Creativity Coach Businesses to Open

6. 32 Podcasting & Other Businesses to Open Showing People How to Cut Expenses

7. 35 Video Podcasting Careers and Businesses to Start

8. 801 Action Verbs for Communicators

9. A Perfect Mitzvah Gift Book

10. A Private Eye Called Mama Africa

11. Ancient and Medieval Teenage Diaries

12. Anne Joan Levine, Private Eye

13. Astronauts and Their Cats

14. Cleopatra's Daughter

15. Counseling Anarchists

48. Job Coach-Life Coach-Executive Coach-Letter & Resume-Writing Service

49. Large Print Crossword Puzzles for Memory Enhancement

50. Make Money with Your Camcorder and PC: 25+ Businesses

51. Middle Eastern Honor Killings in the USA

52. Murder in the Women's Studies Department

53. New Afghanistan's TV Anchorwoman .

54. Nutritional Genomics - A Consumer's Guide to How Your Genes and Ancestry Respond to Food

55. One Day Some Schlemiel Will Marry Me, Pay the Bills, and Hug Me.

56. Popular Health & Medical Writing for Magazines

57. Power Dating Games

58. Predictive Medicine for Rookies

59. Problem-Solving and Cat Tales for the Holidays

60. Proper Parenting in Ancient Rome

61. Roman Justice: SPQR

62. Sacramento Latina

63. Scrapbooking, Time Capsules, Life Story Desktop Videography & Beyond with Poser 5, CorelDRAW ® Graphics Suite 12 & Corel WordPerfect Office Suite 12

64. Search Your Middle Eastern and European Genealogy

89. Traveling Poems and Short Stories. Published both in paperback and as an e-book by lulu.com. See: http://www.lulu.com/content/3879306.

90. Do You Have the Aptitude & Personality to Be A Popular Author?

INDEX